Who's Schooling Who?

Looking for the wizard behind the curtain who can answer questions on education for students, teachers and parents.

Edited By

Ushanda Pauling, Veronica Blakely *and* Lynnette Stallworth

P.B.S. Publishers
Tampa Bay Florida
www.wisw.net
info@wisw.net

Who's Schooling Who?©

P.B.S. Publishers, Tampa Bay Florida

Copyright MMX (2010). All rights reserved.

Copyright MMX (2010) P.B.S. Publishers (1-529423101)

ISBN: 978-0-692-01247-5

Cover and Interior Design by Floyd Smith
P.B.S. Publishers Logo from original art work of William Nathaniel Webb 1969

DEDICATION

To God be the glory for placing the vision of **Who's Schooling Who?** in us.

Our offering is a salute to all educators.

Applause and thanks to those who have long championed the work of education.

We are particularly mindful of teachers of ancient time to now, and those teachers of the future. We give honor to ancestors who taught through oral teaching who shaped our hearts and minds and keep our spirits hopeful… even now.

For all children who hunger and thirst for the basics of education and are open to be guided by wisdom, we need to listen to them. We ask them to give us yet another chance to do better.

APPRECIATION

It has been our good fortune to have been supported and encouraged throughout this process of writing and publishing by many friends, family members, neighbors, and businesses. We are grateful to one another for the extraordinary collaboration we have shared and enjoyed. While our work sessions may have been viewed by others looking in as having an "all day recess," we successfully balanced having fun with getting the work done.

Courtney Smith and Mark Stallworth generously gave "The Book Project" a most comfortable and attractive place to meet and work. Thank you to all at Smith and Stallworth Law Firm for your active support.

Special Thanks

> *Then there is a heartfelt word of gratitude to Mark and Selena Stallworth and Mason Andrew for their generous sponsorship. Likewise we thank T & J and Budd whose sponsorship put the book project on solid ground. Once again life has taught the caring from friends and family makes all the difference in the world!*

With sincere gratitude,
Ushanda, Veronica and Lynnette.

DISCLAIMER

Who's Schooling Who? is a compilation. The editors and publishers are not held responsible for the individual writings or opinions of the contributing authors or interviewees.

The thoughts, experiences, and positions taken are solely those of the specific writer or interviewee.

The surveys reflected upon are a minimal cross-section of students, teachers and, parents/guardians. They are meant to flavor and further the conversation regarding education transformation. The surveys are in no way used as a formal scientific study.

The opinions expressed are not necessarily those of others associated with this offering.

INTRODUCTION

Welcome! Welcome to "The Book Project". **Stop,** don't get nervous there is not a major typo and you have the right book.

"The Book Project" had been the working title. In the beginning what was known was the book's objective. The intention was and still is **to make a positive contribution to the emerging national conversation concerning education.**

As the book was being refined **three realizations** became apparent. We realized education impacts each and every person without exception. Education is a life-long fact. **Education is with us from the cradle to the grave.** Learning is as essential as breathing in and breathing out.

The next realization was the magnitude of education on our lives. It influences virtually every aspect of living on a daily basis. Imagine not being educated enough to read, write and do simple mathematics.

There came the third realization. To the *best of our knowledge and research* this book is the **first comprehensive compilation written to reflect diverse voices on the matter of education in America.**

It has long been said and believed '......an army runs on its stomach....;' meaning an essential need is sufficient food to fuel the troops. What then does a nation and society run on? The belief in this book is that a nation runs on its intellect and character; heart and spirit plus the basics of food and shelter. All of these elements are gained by and through education.

From these three realizations the title for this offering emerged and the focus was clarified. Given the changes in the world and our living in the 21st Century, education begs to be updated and upgraded. Education has changed. Changes over time were subtle as well as overt. They have been deliberate and accidental. Education requires all to exam prior goals and future directions.

Is there any wonder that education is in crisis? At the very center of it all there comes the question: **"Who's Schooling Who?"** It is from this question another layer appeared, leading to many, many more questions.

- Is the current educational system sensitive to what students are trying to tell directly and indirectly to educators?

- How, what, where does systemic change take place? Standardizing this and that appear irrational for a diverse nation.

- Is the current educational system simply outdated or broken altogether? There seems to be the possibility of both given the strong signal set by two consecutive Presidents.

  - Bush's – "No child left behind" (NCLB)
  - Obama's – "Race to the top" (R2T)

- Are the *inmates* running the *asylum*? The rules seem to be made based on "customer service" concepts. The students (and parents) are the new customers in education these days.

We could continue listing pieces of the problem. At some point the crisis in education somewhat resembles the characters in The Wizard of Oz. They are wandering, scattered, unsure, fearful, incoherent and lost. They agree the solution is held by the Wizard, thus begins their search to find all answers to all questions.

And so it is, **Who's Schooling Who?** is in part looking for "The Wizard behind the curtain" who can answer these questions and more to renew, redesign, revive and transform education for students, teachers, parents and all stakeholders.

Rest assured we do not believe we have "the" answers, but we are saying we have questions, ideas, and observations that may lead to better results.

The manner in which we have chosen to present the questions, ideas and observations is important. Our hope is that you'll experience **Who's Schooling Who?** as a comfortable and accessible read. There will not be intentional blaming. There will be raising questions in straightforward ways, sounding the alarm and inviting all to participate. Suggestions will be highlighted in most cases at the end of the author's writing.

Who's Schooling Who? is not a technical or theoretical writing; yet it is to be taken as an intelligent engaging, reflective, prophetic and thoughtful work. These are voices with important input to the issues concerning the reshaping of education.

And finally – the point of it all. The reasons we have written this book are to:

- Collect in one place a comprehensive work that focuses on education from many angles.

- Share a variety of personal and professional experiences and expertise that give insight to the current conversation.

- Invite you, the reader to make your voice heard in your own way. Education matters to every one of us one way or another. Dr. Seuss taught us in "Horton Hears a Who" *every*one's voice matters and it takes all of us at the same time to make the life-saving difference.

Journey now down the yellow brick road into **Who's Schooling Who?!** Have pen and paper (old school), laptop, Smartphone (new school) or iPad® (hint of future school) ready. You will want to make notes, raise questions and develop suggestions.

We hope **Who's Schooling Who?** gets you excited – if not excited become curious – if not curious – argumentative. Whatever your response to this book the goal is for you to find yourself fully engaged in education transformation now.

On behalf of the Editors, Contributing Authors, and Interviewers we are glad you're here.

Lynnette Stallworth
Editor-in-Chief, Who's Schooling Who?

TABLE OF CONTENTS

🍎 **Bookmarks** 🍎

A gift to you from "Who's Schooling Who?"
www.whoisschoolingwho.com
www.wisw.net

"One hundred years from now..."
an excerpt from Forest Witcraft

x

SEMESTER I
School's In

Thank You!

WOW! What A Day!

To start with:

The News coming on campus to do a story about our dismissal challenges.

Four classes stuck out in portables.

Torrential rain causing us to go to plan B (cameras rolling).

A leak in the roof where we were putting kids in plan B (switch to plan C, cameras rolling).

Busses not able to get to the pick up.

Did I mention torrential rain (add lightning warnings)?

Ms. G. slips and falls on the concrete (she's ok cameras rolling)!

Fire alarm goes off/ a decision to be made whether or not to evacuate the building. Did I mention torrential rain & lightning? (camera getting wet...they left!)

Angry parent upset because we did not let him know the bus was going to be late.

Angry parent yells at teacher wants to talk to me.

I yell at angry parent. (not good)

Call my director to expect a call.

Fire Department shows up. Generator and portable problems.

The power goes off in the building!

The curtain falls, the steel curtain in the office (nobody was hurt).

The silver lining:

The folks from (The News) saw a team of people come together and made a comment to one of our parent volunteers that they couldn't believe how a team of people came together

Getting wet but keeping their kids safe.

I guess they didn't know we like to play in the rain...and that we are dedicated to our jobs.

It is a pleasure to work with such an awesome inspiring group of people like you.

Thanks
Anonymous, School Principal, August 2010

An Interview with Psychologist, Denise Lindsay-Blue

with Ushanda Pauling

Please share an occasion when you were "schooled" by a student?

I worked as an Associate Psychologist at a school based mental health facility in a lower income area of New York City (NYC). As part of the summer program, we would go on trips with the goal of expanding the worldview and experiences of the children. During one planned trip, the bus was late and the children were waiting for an extended period of time. I thought it would be nice if we played some games or sang songs while we waited, to make time pass quickly. I started to sing some songs that I sang as a child when I went to camp. It did not go well. I did not understand why. So I became persistent telling them to try something new and it really was fun once they got started. One of the boys looked at me shook his head and said, "This ain't no sleep away camp…we're here in NYC standing on the hot sidewalk, and we're not going to sing those songs no matter how hard you try to sell them to us." What he was trying to tell me was to stay in the here and now and to accept his reality and be there in the moment before trying to change his experience. What he preferred to do at that time was talk to me, and when I met him where he was at that moment, I was able to make a real connection instead a forced experience of pseudo-relatedness or my idea of what his childhood experiences should be.

What is the single best change that could be made to improve the current educational system?

I think the most important change that could be implemented is to stop thinking that there is one answer to effect significant change in our children's lives. The problem is multi-faceted, therefore different approaches and different resources will be needed at different times.

However, I am intrigued by a concept introduced in Malcolm Gladwell's book entitled *Outliers: The Story of Success*. Building upon his idea of grouping children together based on their age and stage of development;

I would divide the children based on whether they had late or early birthdays. The premise being that, children who were physically smaller or less developed socially, motorically, and cognitively would not have to compete for resources against those children with later birthdays who are further along in attaining developmental milestones.(1)

I think the one single change that would have the best effect would be to raise the salaries of educators so that the field would attract the brightest and the most talented of the college pool. In the past, when many scientific fields and corporate America were closed to women, America benefitted by having some of the greatest minds in the classroom because there was nowhere else for women to pursue challenging careers. Fortunately, times have changed (for the most part) but with this change, America lost some of their brightest minds as educators. Of course, we don't want to go back in time but something has to be done to make teaching an honorable and well compensated profession.

In what ways was school administration added to or taken away from successful learning?

The emphasis on standardized testing and prepping for test has taken on a life of its own. Exploration, creative thinking, and inferential thinking has been sucked out of the educational experience. I think that school administration has forgotten the joy of discovery. I think the current administration has created a significant amount of children who are ridden with anxiety because they are scheduled to take tests and another bunch of children who are frozen by their anxiety and decide it is just easier to give up.

Inferential, deductive and creative reasoning skills are so important because they are the basic skills needed to think critically. Someone who is able to think critically is willing to, and can tolerate engaging in mental tasks that are complex and challenging. The critical thinker exhibits open-mindedness and flexibility. They are more apt to work out of the box and see solutions. The critical thinker not only thinks and challenges his and other's thoughts because (s)he can, but learns to find purpose in his/her thinking.

I remember when I was teaching a General Psychology course, a student asked, "Why do we have to learn all of this stuff and take tests?" She further reasoned that, "All of the information we need is on the internet; asking us to learn all of this material is a waste of our time." I responded, "Without a basic understanding of this material, how would you know what questions to ask on the internet" and given all of the contradictory information on the internet; how would you know whether the information was from a credible source?" Sadly her response was, "Oh!" I would have loved a debate or heated informed argument. Nothing followed.

Given the increasing debate concerning education, what are matters/issues you believe imperative to contribute to the debate?

Until adequate funding is provided to attract the best in the field and all children are seen as a priority, positive change cannot occur.

Can the current system be rehabilitated or is a new construct required?

Many errors have been made but we have learned a great deal from our mistakes. Do we toss everything out – even the lessons learned – to start anew? Or do we build upon the knowledge gained by our missteps? All or nothing thinking can be dangerous and costly.

How would you restructure the educational system?

Allow me to list my thoughts on reforming the current educational system:

I think that Gladwell, may have something when he speaks of grouping children by age but also by dividing them into subgroups that consist of early birthdays and later birthdays; at least, in the earlier grades. The reason behind this being those children who are developmentally more immature would not be competing against those children who excel merely because they are older. (1)

    i.   Cross grade, cross school mentoring- creating learning hubs where older can mentor and tutor younger is a wonderful way to reinforce learning and also strengthen the sense of community, while reducing negative behaviors.

ii.   Breakdown the barriers that prevent parents from participating in their children's learning. Use technology to allow for video conferencing parent- teacher meetings or as a means to see what their children are learning.

iii.   Bring back neighborhood schools with high quality teachers so that children can interact with their peers in and out of the classroom.

iv.   Include holistic approaches of mental health into school curriculum, such as deep breathing, yoga, and mindfulness meditation.

What is your understanding of the goal of education?

When school was originally created for the masses, its goal was to produce compliant moral citizens who would be able to read and understand the laws of the land and the King James Bible. It was believed that order and civility would be maintained if immigrants and the lower rung of society and their children were able to understand the laws of man and God. Even for the chosen and the privileged few who were selected to pursue higher education, the goal of their education was to prepare them to be stewards of the Bible and the laws of the land for future generations. Education was not meant to promote individualistic thinking but to encourage personal sacrifice for God, the community, and the nation.

As the age of technology passed to the age of information, the goals of education changed; but not as much as one would think. The goal of education for our nation, at large, is to maintain a competitive edge in the world economy and create citizens who are willing to forgo their individual needs when it is in opposition to the greater goal of the United States.

In creating and implementing this master plan of educating the masses, something very different has happened. The masses began to use education as a tool to "question" the status quo and to create the "privilege" that they were neither born into nor wealthy enough to buy.

The nation has now come to experience a very challenging dilemma.

Should the nation spend its resources and create educational goals that provide opportunity for the masses that may or may not benefit the nation's agenda, or does it spend the majority of its resources on and create goals for the most promising, talented and gifted few? I think education continues to grapple with this question.

What are lessons families and/or students have taught you about learning?

As a Developmental Specialist, I assessed infants by looking at their cognitive, motor and language development. Upon testing infants across different ethnicities I found something interesting. When I worked in Los Angeles, I found many of the recently immigrated Mexican babies to be slower in their motor development than Caucasian and African-American babies of the same age. If I were to take a cursory look at the results I could make the assumption that their parents were not providing a stimulating environment for their children because of lack of interest or knowledge and subsequently I would stress how important it was to allow the child to have floor time and to play and explore his/her environment. I shared, by doing this parents could ensure a healthy outcome for the child. I knew Latin mothers tended to be very family centered and nurturing; what I found out was that the houses they lived in had dirt floors with parasites. If the mother had allowed the baby to crawl around the baby would have become sick. So she was actually being a protective mother by not allowing the baby to crawl. The same scenario presented itself when they moved to California. Mom would have been negligent to let the baby crawl around with floor hazards. I gave strategies to address safety hazards but to be able to provide motor development opportunities for the baby. This was one of the most profound experiences that changed my approach to working with families. It helped me in my therapy and in teaching. Again the lesson became clear; begin where the family is and to ask why.

In your opinion, what are the significant factors for successful learning?

I think a better question would be, "How do we get our children to think?" If we provide opportunities for children to think, learning will occur naturally. Thinking is defined as "the complex act of processing information in a meaningful way that comes from our senses, emotions, and memories." This ability allows us to engage in higher order reasoning, problem solving and creativity. Presenting opportunities and environments that encourage our children to think will exponentially produce learning.

Unfortunately, there is a trend taking place in early education that I find counterintuitive to learning. That is, introducing curriculum earlier and earlier. Remember back, in kindergarten you played; what parents and some educators have forgotten is that play is important for learning. Play is learning. Playing house teaches social skills and planning. Playing with blocks teaches spatial relations and mathematics (quantitative and qualitative). Drawing with crayons helps with fine motor development and planning; drawing with crayons is a precursor to writing with a pencil. Time on the playground helps with balance, coordination and understanding of visual perspective and depth perception. While the child is playing, (s) he is thinking, problem solving and using creativity. All of these skills are essential for success in later years.

I also think we need to go to the metric system for math. One of the things researchers have been looking at and questioning is, why our children are lagging in mathematical abilities versus other industrialized nations? Those nations use the same unit of 10 across all subjects from grade one to college. American children learn measurements using one system, time using another, and computation using another system. We have a different language for numbers. We have these different ways to teach math, instead of one basic unit. We know that the more you use something the more comfortable and competent you become with it. So it's not that other countries are better in math it's that they have had more time and practice with the same system of measurement from day one.

Middle School

Another disturbing trend is having students choose career paths as early as Junior High School. Based on what we know about child development, this is an age where students should be taking calculated risks and exploring their likes and dislikes. To pigeon hole a student at this crucial stage of developmental exploration thwarts their sense of curiosity, exploration, and the important lessons that are learned by making mistakes, bad decisions, or turning in to blind alleys. This is where they should be exposed to as many choices as possible.

At this stage of development, it is supposed to be okay for adolescents to not know who they are. There are undiscovered talents yet to be developed that are stifled by this new system of having students choose career paths in the middle grades. To be perfectly clear, I am not talking about getting rid of the concept of introducing students to career choices.

My way would be to have various career tracks in each school and for students to rotate similar medical interns so there would be a cycle of different career emphasis. This could be done by school year, nine weeks, trimester, however. The goal being to expose them to as many options as possible so that they not necessarily know the directions they would like to explore but more so eliminating those choices that are the least appealing.

High School

Some high schools have it right. The high schools that have integrative learning in which regardless of the subject area the topic is the same, for example, if material about Egypt is taught in a geography class, other subjects like physics and math are also talking about Egypt as it relates to that subject. What we know about learning is that when it is relevant it is easier to take in (referred to as learning modules); teachers work together and decide what the topic is so that each subject will pertain to the chosen topic. The class time is longer so that you can have time to discuss, explain, and do interactive activity; using different mediums. Teaching a civics lesson then taking kids to an election; not just talking about it. Schools that are doing that are doing it right; where there is technology to assist them; time set aside to discuss with peers and run ideas against each other.

Teaching is a very isolated experience and there isn't time to collaborate or time for new teachers to learn from more seasoned teachers. Additionally, problems lie in impoverished areas that don't have the resources and students can't even take books home. What we know about learning is that the more senses we use, the better we understand and the more we retain. We are setting students up to fail if we teach them something in class without allowing them time to review and read for themselves. For everything we know about memory and learning there is not a consistent approach in impoverished areas.

Does the current battery of testing (and scoring) help students learn? If yes, how/what?

The purpose of formal testing is to assess where a student is functioning, to learn about strengths and weaknesses, and to help create modes of instruction. Testing does not help someone to learn. I believe that testing is being misused and not used to assist the student or improve the educational process. Tests are a very good tool when used appropriately. However, when tests are used to label, track children or hinder learning then the true usefulness of testing is not being utilized. Changing tests, eliminating tests or moving to a portfolio system is not the answer. The answer lies in the bigger question of redefining what our goals are in education.

"Testing is not meaningful, unless everyone in the system – schools, teachers, students – are held accountable for the results of the test. Not everything that is valuable in education can be measured in tests. But when students cannot demonstrate in tests the knowledge and skills expected of them that is now a warning sign that triggers intense corrective action.

Tom Horne, former Superintendent State of Arizona Schools

An Interview with Irene B. Johnston

A Seasoned Teacher of 35 Years
in Elementary School Education
with Lynnette Stallworth

For you, Irene what changes in education have been most dramatic?

The focus on testing under the current system has created an environment that is more pressure packed than ever before, for both students and teachers. Teaching has become a "pressure-keg"!

What was teaching prior to the increased testing?

Teaching had been curriculum based on needs of students, that was the number one priority. The curriculum is now based on the benchmarks by which students are to be evaluated.

Please say more about the benchmarks?

It has become an "upward" shift. A Kindergartener was a Kindergartener. Now a Kindergartner is expected to be a first grader. By that I mean what had been Kindergarten benchmarks are now first grade benchmarks based on "Florida Sunshine State Standards".(2) The risk is students starting out the-gate already behind. There are far too many children without opportunity for voluntary pre-K on Head-start or any programs before entering the public education system. They come into education already behind. Some children come in with reading readiness already established, while others have little experience in the areas of reading. Many have never had a book or held a pencil.

How does testing impact your teaching?

Way too much testing! From the first day of a new school year it is all about testing! Some students do not test well. This places a real strain on both me as a teacher and for my students, the ones who test well and the ones who don't test well.

What would you use in place of testing?

I would be excited to have a national norm test for students; not a state only test.

I also believe teachers should be evaluated on all levels, aspects of teaching - at the end of the school year. If the teacher has a good evaluation then they should have only one observation the next year. For those who have some problems they certainly should be helped by monitoring with more than one observation; along with support to quickly improve.

Your school district, Hillsborough County (HCPS) was awarded a substantial grant called "Empowering Effective Teachers". It was originally called the Gates Grant. What is your understanding of its intent?

"Empowering Effective Teachers" is a Bill and Melinda Gates Foundation Grant. This differs from Mark Zuckerberg's (CEO & Founder of Facebook) million dollar challenge grant.

Basically I understand the purpose is trying to help teachers be the best teacher they can be. And as far as I know, we (HCPS) are the only county that received this grant in the state of Florida.

How does it work?

There is a mentor, the principal, and assistant principal. They are specially trained to do evaluations. Appointments are made before hand with each teacher for a pre-interview, an observation and a post-interview.

The teacher being evaluated has a choice of the lesson to be observed. A standard questionnaire is completed by the teacher beforehand that gives an overview of the lesson to be presented. Most teachers are observed a minimum of two times by the mentor, depending on the outcome of previous evaluations.

If the teacher does not have a previous evaluation such as a first-year teacher or transfer teacher they will have several more observations.

Every teacher also has an observation done by the principal. If more observations are required the assistant principal may do some of the needed evaluations.

Would you like to see the pre-observation question?

Yes, thanks.

These are the pre-observation questions:

1. What is your lesson objective?

2. How is/are the lesson objective(s) aligned with state curriculum standards?

3. What data did you use to design lesson? How did the data influence the planning of the lesson?

4. How will you know if your lesson was/were achieved?

5. What teaching strategies will you use to teach this lesson? What resources will be utilized.

6. Why did you choose these strategies and resources?

7. What is the academic relationship between this lesson with past or future lessons (why this lesson? why now?)

8. Please explain any special situations or circumstances of which the observer might need to be aware.

9. The observer will provide feedback on this lesson. Are there specific areas you would like the observer to look for/focus on?

How are the evaluations scored?

There are rankings. A teacher is ranked by points as 0 to 3.

    0 = Requires Action (little knowledge)

    1= Developing (some awareness of important concepts)

    2= Accomplished (solid knowledge)

    3= Exemplary (extensive knowledge)

There are four categories that are measured called "Domains"

    Domain 1 - Planning and Preparation

Domain 2 - Classroom Environment

Domain 3 - Instruction

Domain 4 - Professional Responsibility

What happens after the observation?

The post observation is by appointment. The teacher and the evaluator meet. I was told by observer what was liked, not liked and areas of improvement. I was asked if I could have done better or anything differently. I was not told my overall ranking. Your ranking is sent to you by e-mail.

Who are the mentors? And how does someone become a mentor?

Former teachers that have gone through this special training. A couple of problems for me is some mentors are not grading consistently and some mentors have never taught at the grade levels they observe. And some mentors have never taught the subject matter being evaluated. Yet these individuals do the serious and sometimes severe work of determining a teacher's value and fate.

Where are mentors being found?

If you are asking how mentor search and hiring is done, I'm not sure. There was an e-mail and online posting within the county system. Who sees those I can't say. I have not seen any posting for the position in the local media.

What has been your experience of "Empowering Teachers" up to now?

As a seasoned teacher I have a sense of what first-year teachers must go experience. It was unnerving and anxiety provoking! The previous evaluating process, "Empowering Teachers" was not the best, but clearly this isn't either.

I believe a good teacher knows they are good they don't need someone to tell them. A teacher having difficulty needs help. Those are the ones who need attention. Teachers doing well should be left to do their job. Testing and new evaluation program has put pressure that is unbelievable. There is intense scrutiny on the entire teaching profession. The morale among the rank and file is awful. The morale is as low as I've experienced in thirty-five years of teaching!

Have you any idea of other teacher's experiences with the grant's evaluation?

Because we've talked to one another I have heard quite a bit from other colleagues. Teachers talking with teachers for example I was told two classrooms were set up identically; the very same way. One was given feedback; the room poorly setup. The other teacher was told it was a good set up! The rooms were exactly the same and the same mentor!

Other teachers have asked what they could do to improve their skills, some mentors simply have no answers or suggestions to offer.

On the day the Physical Education teacher was to have his observation it happened to have rained. He decided to use an indoor room. He was told he was marked down for 'poor student's space.' It was not his fault that it rain…

Can you share any praise or concern about your evaluation experience?

I wish I could say something honestly good about this grant evaluation process. I wish I really could place the program in a more positive light. Unfortunately the push-back from the teachers was overwhelming. The program needs to be reworked in several areas.

I can tell you my first observation I was told there would be very few exemplary rankings. I hunch they want to start low in order to show improvement for teachers which then will reflect well for "Empowering Teachers." It makes a better appearance on the program to have progression versus regression. If the teacher ranks high on the first evaluation where would they go from there?

If what you say is a factor, what is your overall interpretation of the evaluation?

At best it is questionable. How can data be useful when observers are very inconsistent, mentors are not grading consistently mentors are not fully equipped to be observers.

The evaluation process should be standardized.

It would have been smarter to use this first year of "Empowering Teachers" as a trial run.

The first year definitely should have been used as a testing the process.

In my opinion what does is the impact to having a private citizen(s) giving money to evaluate a public system?

It is strange isn't it? It would be odd if a private person or persons gave money without stipulation or strings attached.

What do you see as the future for "Empowering Teachers"?

It is my understanding this year everyone MUST participate in "Empowering Teachers." Next year teachers are allowed to opt out of the program. Opting-out would mean your salary will be from a baseline only. If you stay in the program your evaluation will determine if your salary increases or not. A teacher could make less if their scores are low but not necessarily make more. That's my understanding of the "Empowering Teachers" evaluation.

I think two to three years down-the-road most teachers will opt out.

Given the current state of education, what are immediate changes you would encourage?

1. Bring discipline back into the classroom! Establish real consequences; such as students sent home to parents if expelled from school. Teachers feel their hands are tied. If the word "bully" is mentioned it means more paperwork, not necessarily a change in behavior or consequence for behavior. This leads to the second immediate change.

2. More responsibility to parents! The general sentiment seems to be 'what a child does at home is the parent's business. What a child does at school is the teacher's business.' Parents are not accepting their responsibility.

3. Ultimately, there must be true collaboration and cooperation amongst school, home and community.

Community in the immediate would involve daycare or after school provider.

I have to ask, Irene from your vantage point "who is schooling who?"

Teachers are teaching teachers. We are giving encouragement, guidance and professional support to one another. Teachers are giving loyalty and best efforts to administrators. Teachers are teaching and caring for children. Children are schooling teachers. The system is being run like a corporate business.

Students teach me tolerance and patience, on the worst day a student can make it the best day! "Who's Schooling Who?" should be a full circle if done the right way. The question right now is, "who is there for the teacher?"

SEMESTER II

Take Your Seat

"Forward Only if You Can Read This"

One of the best things to hold onto in this world is your mind

Eonverye taht can raed tihs rsaie yuor hnad.

fi yuo cna raed tihs, yuo hvae a sgtrane mnid too

Cna yuo raed tihs? Olny 55 plepoe out of 100 can.

i cdnuolt blveiee taht I cluod aulaclty uesdnatnrd waht I was rdanieg. The phaonmneal pweor of the hmuan mnid, aoccdrnig to a rscheearch at Cmabrigde Uinervtisy, it dseno't mtaetr in waht oerdr the ltteres in a wrod are, the olny iproamtnt tihng is taht the frsit and lsat ltteer be in the rghit pclae. The rset can be a taotl mses and you can sitll raed it whotuit a pboerlm. Tihs is bcuseae the huamn mnid deos not raed ervey lteter by istlef, but the wrod as a wlohe. Azanmig huh? yaeh and I awlyas tghuhot slpeling was ipmorantt!

Only **great minds** can read this!

SOCIAL PROMOTION

by Veronica Blakely

There was a time, not so long ago, when receiving the grade of "F" on a report card meant that you had failed the class and therefore had to repeat the class. Over the years, that concept has changed drastically in public schools. Retaining a failing student in the same grade has seemingly become taboo. It turns out that for some schools, a student with a failing grade of "F" can be promoted to the next grade level along with other classmates who made an "A". According to public school bureaucracy, this craziness is supposed to help the failing student have a positive self-image, which in turn will help the student perform better at the next grade level. If only that were true, instead the education system has set up a process that allows the failing student to do little if any work in class because the student now knows a promotion to the next grade level will not be denied. This process has come to be known as "social promotion" which allows teachers, students, and parents the opportunity to look the other way while chaos in the educational process is occurring.

Social promotion (said to have started approximately around 1977) is the practice of advancing a student to the next grade level when he or she has not mastered all of the content from the previous grade.(3)   *In 1999, The U.S. Department of Education* referred to social promotion as the practice of allowing students who do not meet grade-level performance standards and academic requirements to pass on to the next grade with their peers. (4) Whichever definition you choose, they both mean failure for students in life as well as in the classroom. To this end, failing students become less motivated to do the required class work because they feel empowered that nothing they do will change the process. While this might be the case for some schools, there are other school districts that are rethinking the process of social promotion.

My concern for social promotion focuses on what is this process supposed to teach students other than that they can "slack" off and still get rewarded. Someone has to know that this behavior, once started, will continue because "slacking" students will possibly turn into "slacking" adults. These students become the people adults who get a job and feel that they can show up to work when they want, do only as much work as they want, and somehow expect to still get paid. It is sad for these individuals who will have to learn the lessons in adulthood that they did not learn in school, everyone must pull their own weight if they want to be rewarded.

What about the parents of these students who are socially promoted? Are they looking at the progress reports and report cards to check the status of their child? Do they attend teacher conferences or Parent Teacher Association (PTA) meetings to stay informed? The obvious answer here is no, because a parent who is involved with their child's education will get the help their child needs so that their child can be successful.

Then there are the teachers who blindly go along with social promotion because they really feel it is best for the students. There are other teachers who do the best they can to help failing students succeed in spite of the bureaucracy they face daily. These are the teachers who suffer from "burn out" and leave the educational system because they know there is little they can do to change it. Yet, these are the teachers we all should want in the classroom to ensure all children get the education they so rightly deserve.

What about the community and their role in social promotion? Sadly, many in the community are not aware that such an animal exist and assume that everything at the local school is going along just fine. This is especially true for those who do not have children in the public school system and/ or do not volunteer at their local public school. I was part of that community who was unaware what was happening in the public school system until I became a high school teacher at an inner city school. I was shocked to find that some students could only read on the 3rd and 4th grade level even though they were enrolled at a high school. Much to my dismay, this was not a problem unique to the school where I taught, but this was a national problem. How could this be possible and who allowed this to happen on such a large scale? A range of emotions clouded my head all at the same time with a singe of anger that someone thought this was an acceptable practice and I should just go with the flow. To add insult to injury, students entering high school had to take and pass the state standardized test when they reached the 10th grade whether they could read on that level or not. Those students who did not pass this test before graduating 12th grade would only receive a "Certificate of Attendance" instead of a high school diploma. Non-diploma students would be allowed to attend summer school to retake the test so that they could obtain their diploma. Unfortunately, many of these students would never return to complete this process which means they attended 12 years of school for naught. Please note that those students who were unsuccessful in passing the state standardized test were remedial as well as non-remedial students.

The saddest part of this process was to see the look on the face of the parents who were surprised to find out their child did not receive a diploma and that the student had failed most of their classes. These parents had paid for invitations, caps and gowns only to find out their child had not successfully completed the credits needed to graduate. The even sadder truth is some of these parents had been socially promoted as well and somehow thought their child was going to be more successful than they were. The question came to mind, "Why did the schools allow these failing students to march in the graduation processional?" The answer goes back to previous answers for social promotion, "They wanted them to have a positive self-image," which was the same reason given as to why these students were not retained when they failed in elementary and middle school. Didn't someone realize once you start a lie you must keep it going until someone has the courage to tell the truth? No one told these students the truth so they helped carry this lie all the way to their graduation day. These students will possibly continue to carry this lie with their children and grandchildren until someone is willing to stand for the truth.

The greatest loss here is to the community at large. We are producing an illiterate society who will be subjected to low paying jobs, public assistance, or incarceration. With schools failing to educate a large part of the population, our country will then become lacking in leaders, teachers, and a literate society. What are we to do to combat this horror and stop the bleeding from this wound? We all must get involved. If you can read, teach someone else how to read. If you are good at math, teach someone how to solve basic and complicated equations; volunteer at schools, community centers, churches, or wherever there is a tutoring program. This is a national problem and we must take national action in order to raise the educational standards of our country. We cannot sit on the sidelines and think this is not our problem because we do not have a child in the public school system. Our lives will be impacted by these socially promoted students whether we like it or not. Those of us paying taxes will pay into a system that will either give public assistance, pay for incarceration, or other social maladies that await this uneducated population. Let us choose to educate instead of incarcerate; it is our duty.

HOW THE STUDENTS SCHOOLED ME

For three years I was a high school teacher. I learned numerous things about education and the public school system. However, the lessons learned from the students were the most profound. I learned that students were dealing with a different set of challenges in 2005 than what I and other students dealt with in 1965. I also learned these students knew how to "game" the system and how some of the students beat the system at its own game.

First, the students schooled me by showing their resilience against all odds. There were a disproportionate number of students who were in crisis situations because they were either homeless, being reared by their siblings or had drug/alcohol addicted parents. Students rearing themselves were less likely to come to school or pay attention when they got there. Some had to work to support their families because the head of household did not make their children a priority. As a teacher, I had to recognize it was difficult for these students to learn if they were hungry, homeless, and helpless while carrying the weight of the world on their shoulders. Compassion in teaching had to be the order of the day when faced with these circumstances.

Surprisingly, these students blended in well with the population of other students. You would not know they were in a crisis situation until an incident occurred or someone told you about their issue(s). Many came to school to escape what awaited them at home, and most of them tried their best to be good students. Some students succeeded without their crisis being detected by others. It was these students who touched a soft spot in your heart and who many teachers would try to help in any way they could. Some stood against the test of time while some others dropped out of school because the pressure was too great. For those who successfully walked across that stage at graduation, they received huge rounds of applause from those of us who knew their struggle. Yes, these students schooled me and other teachers that sometimes you have to be flexible in the classroom with assignments because all students were not functioning from the same set of circumstances.

The second way I was "schooled" was by those students who knew how to "work" the social promotion system. Some schools implemented several options for students to catch up on their classwork, which some students took to mean they did not have to do **any** of their classwork. Students were allowed to sign up for after-school programs, night school, in-school tutoring, and an accelerated learning program to catch up on work the students did not do in class. For some students, this meant they had time to socialize which gave them time to disrupt the class. Of course this was chaotic for the teacher who had to deal with disciplinary issues instead of teaching the lesson.

Many students used these options all the way up to the 12th grade until they were able to take an accelerated term on the computer, covering several subjects. These students were able to do in a couple of months what other students took years doing by paying attention in class, completing their assignments, and passing their tests. Why did someone think this was OK or even fair to the other students who did what they were sent to school to do? Once again, these options were put in place so students would not feel bad because they were not successful in completing their work for each grade level. Students had already learned these options in elementary and middle school, why should high school be any different? These students "schooled" me and other teachers by demonstrating they could come to school every day, do no class work, and be allowed to catch up with their classmates with little to no penalty. These students did not just learn how to make the system work for them, they taught some of their classmates to do the same. The sad part to this is that the students did not try to hide what they were doing and the schools seemed powerless to stop them; because these programs were put in place to help "struggling" students. Who was to say which students were struggling and which were not? In the end, the students had the last laugh because they were able to use the classroom for socializing and other disruptions until they were ready to be "schooled".

How can the education system be so different from when I went to school in times past? We had fewer resources, yet we had teachers and a school system that cared how we were educated. Social promotion has to be put back inside of Pandora's Box because it is not a benefit to anyone, and certainly not to students. If we continue to look the other way, we all will be at fault for a more illiterate society that is soon to come.

"There's No Place Like Home"
by Lynnette Stallworth

Families come in a countless variety of sizes, configurations, colors and types. It is said there are two kinds of families. We have a family of origin; the one we are physically born or adopted into. And there is our family of choice the people; we select over time, places and events.

If at some point-in-time you have asked, "Who are these people?" you'll know that is your family by birth. Eventually every family becomes a modern family as the next generation infuses newness into what was old. With any good fortune our family of birth and family of selection have points of meaningful connection.

The central character, Dorothy in "The Wizard of Oz" (1936) is portrayed as having a 'modern' family. There was her aunt and uncle who functioned as guardians. And so it is even today children come to have other adults than parents function in the rearing role. In some families the rearing code is being filled by another minor. Children are rearing children.

Children by-in-large have not changed; parents and parenting have changed. There was a time families were organized around children. Today it is far more common for American families to be organized around the demands on parents and/or guardians. The driving force seems to be a matter of financial stability and advancement. It takes at least two paychecks to sustain a household. In addition to sustaining a household the desire to give opportunity for a better life is centered on education.

Education for most families is costly right from birth. Childcare to nursery school to pre-school and on there is an added monetary price-tag. The cost only increases. This begins the ties that bind family and education.

Just as families come in a variety of ways, they also function differently one from another. In general, families do what they can do. There is a range of abilities to functioning in and amongst families. Some families are highly functioning; while others are malfunctioned or even dysfunctional. The important thing is having and helping families be healthy – as healthy as they can be. A reliable starting point to a healthy family is healthy adults. The formula would copy to have a healthy baby you need a healthy mother.

It holds a healthy woman makes the odds greater for healthy children and family.

No family is perfect. Every family has challenges; in fact we are all recovering from our childhood. The educational system helps or hurts – adds to or detracts from the health and wellbeing of a families functioning.

A closer look at a family and its' function includes a reasonable concept of the purpose of family. In simplest of terms, let's consider the purpose of family as being 4 P's. The "4 P's of Parenting" are representative of the basic obligation of all parents/guardians. The "4 P's of Parenting:" *Protect, Provide, Prepare and Promote.*

Protect

A parent/guardian has the responsibility to keep a family physically out of harm's way. As is true with the physician's oath (Hippocratic); "…first, do no harm" holds true for parents as well. Parents are to be "safe people" for their children and make home a "safe place".

Physically safeguarding is the obvious and given. There is another requirement of protecting a child which is emotionally. The world will issue enough harsh blows. The family needs to be determined not to "beat up on" a child's feelings intentionally or unintentionally. This means being constantly conscience of how a child is spoken to, as well as how parents speak to one another. Words have power.

A child will become what they are told about themselves. There is a huge difference in telling a child they are "loveable and capable" than "you won't amount to anything" or other negative comments. Words do have power. They can be affirming or demeaning. Remember "sticks 'n stones can break my bones, but names will never hurt me?" It's a lie! Lie!! The truth is, 'hurt people, hurt people.' The proof is seen in the epidemic of bullying. The proof is shown in the increasing numbers of suicide among youngsters.

Parents/guardians are responsible for the tone and tenor in the family.

Provide

The first thing that comes to mind is "a roof over head." The next is providing food and clothing. Yes, there is no questioning parents/guardians must furnish these daily human necessities, and in today's economy fulfilling this task is demanding.

Even though providing housing, food and clothing for family is demanding it is only the beginning of what parents/guardians are asked to do as providers. Providing involves going beyond the four-walls of home. Parents who desire the best for the family also provide opportunities to expose their child to many experiences outside of the home. This may be occasionally or on a regular basis. Experiences could be a trip to a museum or candy factory. Taking a child to work is as an important experience as having a child in a music class or sports activity. There are countless experiences to expose children to outside the home. What is being provided is a chance to apply home-teaching and school-lessons with real-time relevant activity. As a result, children gain self-knowledge as well as knowledge of the activity.

Being a provider of the basics and the experiential gives the child and family a practice close up and personal that becomes internalized for future use.

Prepare

Preparing includes equipping a child with the tools for living. These tools are not only the standards and values for children to become honorable adults; they are also the reason for and how to implement the standards and values.

For example the value of honesty. The tools to implement and support honesty may be learning to *speak up* even when the child makes a mistake or does wrong. Or a tool to express the value of *self-respect* and *self-worth* may be showing a child their own worth by asking for help when needed.

Preparing at this level means parents/guardians take the time to model and instruct at every opportunity. Being a good preparer is more than material, it is the intangible needs as well.

In the infancy years, preparing is mostly waiting, hoping, and encouraging to the next level of development. Parents need 'lesson plans' too. As a child gets older, preparing is being on the ready – even a step ahead. From here on the duty to prepare a child accelerates. By-in-large a parent/guardian becomes a tutor, a life coach in order to ready the child for what comes next in their development. In order to be a tutor, the person must learn before instructing.

Two critical components of parents and guardians preparing a child for a greater chance to a successful life are :

First, wanting the child. This is an emotional, psychological and spiritual issue. It is essential to be 'in place' at conception. Second is having expectations of the child. A child (as is true for all ages) needs to have goals, hopes and dreams to reach for. Expectations set parameters, standards and values in the early formative years.

Lastly, as concerns preparing a child to grow and flourish are these 5 C's. Prepare a child to be Compassionate, Courageous, Competent, Conscious and Consistent in their living.

1. Compassionate is to care and feel for others.
2. Courageous is to be mind and spirit strong and brave.
3. Competent is to be unquestionably able.
4. Conscious is to be present, awake; fully alive.
5. Consistent is to be steady and reliable.

These 5 C's are suggested as benchmarks and internal compass points to support the best of external behavior.

Promote

What may seem easy isn't. Taking a hint from Michael Eisner when he was head of Disney, it was important, "Not to over expose the Mouse." This philosophy is the cornerstone for parents/guardians as they promote their youngster.

In a nutshell, promoting is the pleasure of being your child's #1 cheerleader. It is being your child's fierce advocate. It is being your child's publicist. But here's the catch – when, who and how to be all of the above and more on behalf of your child.

Speaking and acting in the best interest of a child takes unusual discernment, restraint, integrity, dedication and endurance. A bumper-sticker does not equal promoting. Promoting is standing with a child through all circumstances in a way that is honest and helpful. Blaming the child or the school is not promoting. Taking the child's side all of the time is not promoting. Being objective is not easy yet necessary to demonstrate healthy adult maturity while advancing the child's interest.

Some parents talk about their child to the point of boasting. The dangers are many including weighting the child down to live up to unreasonable expectations setting parent/guardian in a potentially "failed" situation. Both lead to a downward spiral. Not to mention boasting will alienate others. To be proud, yes! To boast, no!

Commending a child requires utmost finesse. On one hand the temptation is to be outspoken everywhere, to everyone, all the time. On the other hand is near silence, passive recognition or "that's your job." Neither makes the mark of commending one is overexposure; the other is withholding. This then is the challenge: to be proud without boasting.

The task of promoting is not to boast or be loud about the child's achievements. Promoting is to be thoughtful, seeking good balance, selective steady, consistent and always hopeful of more accomplishments to come.

These 4 P's are carried out within the context of family on a 24/7 basis in a setting generally referred to as "home." Let's be clear – it is the responsibility of parents/guardians to do the work of the 4 P's.

The current educational system requires parents/guardians to enroll children at a specific age to be taught. The exception is proof of home-schooling. Once a child is enrolled into the educational system, family and education create a dynamic that links one to the other. In the best situations the dynamic between the two becomes an active supportive partnership.

What Happens at Home Does Not Stay at Home

As soon as a child is properly enrolled into the educational system it is a "done deal". It is as pronounced: "home and school are wed!" No one says it yet it is lived out as 'for better or worse, sickness and health, richer and poorer...' till (graduation) do us part.

It is long overdue for home and school to change their relationship. It has been a shaky union. Home and school must intentionally become sensitive to each other. They must decide to actively support one another's goals and purpose for the good of "their children."

There was a time a note from the teacher was enough to summon a parent/guardian immediately to school. And there once was a time a teacher knew the family and the family's functioning level enough to offer authentic support. In recent times both scenarios have dissolved – a bad union.

The times have changed enough that major life altering events are happening to children and neither home nor school can be counted on by the child. Children are experiencing crisis and chaos at home. They go from home to a school system that is broken. How much worse does it have to get for American youngsters?

Today youngsters are having to deal with not only an assortment of abuse, but parents in jail, at war or being homeless. More women are imprisoned in America than ever before.' "War is a curse because it scars people for life," as a veteran puts it. And homeless shelters now have their own bus routes; each has an unmerciful price tag for children.

Children deal with every life issue adults are in – death and dying, birth and pregnancy plus all the points in between. Those children whose parents return from war also share the scars of the soldier.

They both are fighting to regain balance and their humanity. More women – mothers are going to prison than ever in U.S. history. The burden of shame borne by their children is immeasurable.

At school children are stressed by the constant demands of testing not to forget social-peer pressure, and concerns of violence. They are getting ready for state tests. They are taking tests. Teachers are stressed; after all, their jobs are likely to be on the line if the testing doesn't go well. Where do you suppose a teacher's stress in the classroom goes? Is it any wonder children need stress management? The Hawn Foundation is dedicated to teaching children how to be happier. Question is, who is centered enough to take a child for their services?

There's no place like home. There's no place like school. The time is now. Now is the time to wake from this dreadful callous sleep, education and home are in. It is said, 'we don't change because we see the light. We change because we feel the heat.'

"Heat" has been placed on teachers. It is yet to be seen if attaching test scores to teacher evaluations will benefit the system. It is more likely "heat" is needed on the other partner too. Let's reframe "heat" to mean accountability. Accountability on teachers and on parents/guardians is a balanced equation.

Suggested here is the accountability for parent/guardian. Repeatedly, it is reported students who do well have parents/guardians who participate in their schooling. And repeatedly it is reported parents are inadequately showing up for conferences let alone social events. Sad to say, parents/guardians are education "drop-outs", habitually absent for their student.

Given there are rules and laws concerning truancy, absent without permission from school, why not apply regulations with consequences for parents/guardians who do not come to a specific number of conferences? Ensure a consequence to the parent/guardian not the student, when they do not participate in a specific number of voluntary opportunities. It's time we take the student out of the middle of the teacher parent/guardian struggle.

We are setting a high standard for students (that's what testing is about, isn't it?). Time has come to have a respectable standard for parents/guardians; a word about consequence. Hopefully a signed pledge at enrollment will be sufficient. The good ol', 'my word is my bond' approach.

Should the pledge to participate fail, the next attempt might have to be a fine. The fine could be double-duty or when all else fails, the consequence of a monetary penalty with funds remaining in the student's class. Certainly available to transform this aspect of education can be legislation set out by boards of education.

These measures may well be the start of a new day all around. There is no place as good as home when done well. There is no better place for offering quality education as our schools can become.

Character

I would have all young persons taught to respect themselves, their citizenship, the rights of others and all sacred things; to be healthy, industrious, persevering, provident, courteous, just and honest; neat in person and in habit, clean in thought and in speech; modest in manner, cheerful in spirit and Masters of themselves, faithful to every trust, loyal to every duty; magnanimous in judgment, generous in service and sympathetic toward the needy and unfortunate; for these are the most important things in life and this is not only the way of wisdom, happiness and true success, but the way to make the most of themselves and to be of the greatest service to the world.

Albert Norton Parlin

These words are engraved in stone on front wall of the Albert N. Parlin Junior High School in Everett, Massachusetts

"Intelligence Plus Character..."
Moral and Ethics
by John C. Harvey

"Intelligence plus character – that is the goal of a true education."
Dr. Martin Luther King, Jr.

There is no doubt that education in America is at a crossroads. But some of the difficulty is not just attributed to the decline in academics. Even though America has fallen in terms of test scores and academic proficiency, we have also fallen in the area of ethics and morals. We can no longer ignore the reality that America's schools are producing a plethora of students who lack moral fiber and deep ethical convictions.

One can't help but wonder how we have arrived at this current place. How did things dissolved at such a rapid rate? I was sharing a story recently of someone who looked down at the floor in her home and noticed three ants. She said to herself, "it's only three ants, nothing to worry about." She did nothing. The next day when she looked down, she saw six ants. She said to herself, "it's only six ants, nothing to worry about." She did nothing. The next day when she looked down the floor was covered with ants, too numerous to count. She was very upset and wondered why all the ants were there. She had never seen so many ants in the house. She couldn't figure out why the ants were so plentiful. How did this happen? Of course, primarily it happened because nothing was done when she first saw three ants and then six ants. Because she didn't address the problem when it first started, it grew into a much larger and more difficult problem.

This is where we find ourselves currently in American education. When students first began to widely exhibit disappointing behavior, as a society we did nothing. We tolerated students mistreating other students. We tolerated students disrespecting teachers. We tolerated students telling administrators that they can't physically restrain them or discipline them without getting in trouble themselves. And now we have wholesale chaos and confusion in America's schools. Every type of mean-spirited, abusive, and abrasive behavior can be witnessed within American schools.

For instance, bullying has become a national epidemic. Many students dread going to school because somebody is going to tease them, shun them, or make them feel horrible. This type of behavior is no longer confined to the classroom, hallway or the playground. Now they will follow the student online to further agitate and aggravate them. Some students have felt so tortured and troubled by bullies they have taken their own lives. In fact, this has happened with increasing regularity with each passing year. It is time this country takes a careful look at bullying and the numerous other issues that affect American education.

What we currently find is that schools are not just failing in producing academically competent students, but failing in producing moral and ethical students as well. If one begins to focus on many of the issues that face America's schools, they will discover our problems have as much to do with morality and ethics as academics. Many districts find themselves having to address issues such as bullying (including cyber bullying), sexting (which is sending explicit nude photographs over the cell phone or computer), drug and alcohol abuse, teenage pregnancy, and even students disrespecting teachers and administrators. These issues exist independently of whether a student can read, write and do arithmetic. You can even have students who excel academically, yet are involved in some of the issues stated. This should raise for us a whole new set of questions. For instance, everyone wants to see America's students with basic academic competencies. But is academic competency enough considering some of the current realities? If a person has little or no regard for their fellow classmate, is that acceptable as long as they can pass certain tests? If a person can score a 1400 on the SAT exam, but has no problem making fun of another student because of something about them that is different, is that to be tolerated? If a student can read and write but threatens teachers and staff members, is that permissible?

It would appear we have reached the point where schools must make the conscious effort to promote ethics and morality amongst the student body. This means that schools must engage students to think critically and reflectively on what it means to be a moral and ethical person. If this is not done, we will see further decline.

One of the first things that has to happen to improve the overall educational outlook is that America must support educators having control in the classroom. There are too many students who have figured out that they can act out however they want with little to no consequences. As a society, we have tolerated bad and unacceptable behavior because it was emanating from a young person. This has to stop. When teachers witness bad behavior from a student, they must know that they have the authority to handle the situation, without being turned into a villain for doing so. When adults allow children to act as they want, they create the atmosphere for disaster. We have to recognize that our hands off, do not restrain or restrict approach to classroom management has resulted in out of control classes. Every school district should make it perfectly clear that their teachers and administrators have the right to maintain order, civility and respect in the classroom. If this was promoted throughout the country, we might begin to see a shift in certain behavior.

I am aware that whenever you talk about teachers having the authority to maintain order, some will immediately want to raise the issue of the "rights" of students. Those who do so need to be reminded that students have the right to respect others, the right to follow rules, the right to be humane, and the right to learn. When a student stops doing any one of these things, teachers and administrators should have the right to correct them. Without that level of commitment coming from school districts, the current chaos is likely to escalate. Of course, the irony is that most citizens would strongly welcome and support more orderly classrooms and schools, but rarely is their input or opinion solicited. Most people recognize that if you can't keep students in the seats, can't keep them from cursing and berating each other, and can't keep them from hitting and hurting one another, then it is highly unlikely they are having an optimum educational experience.

As one who values and appreciates my educational journey, I am saddened to see what many students have to endure in this current social climate. I recognize how different my time in school was compared to today's students.

In fact, my parents were determined I have the best education possible. I am the youngest son of two parents who are both educators. My mother was a certified teacher. And my father was a certified teacher, vice-principal,

principal, area administrator, and central office administrator.

Learning was a natural part of my childhood. There seemed to be a constant and unbreakable stream of learning that took place both in school and in the home. My parents wanted me to soak up as much knowledge as possible. They also wanted me to be a moral and ethical human being. There were many discussions on the appropriate ways to treat people, the benefits of kindness and compassion, the value of being concerned for the weak and the helpless, and the beauty of generosity. Some of my teachers stressed many of the same ideas by their example in the classroom.

However, much is different in the current social landscape. Because so many students are faced with all sorts of attacks on their dignity, it is important that ethics and morals make a comeback. The modern classroom must also become the place where deeper questions of human interaction get explored. As this occurs, there will be many students who start to evaluate their own behavior in new ways. For instance, some students have never entertained the question, "What does it mean to be a moral person?" Exploring this question will inevitably lead to a whole host of other questions. Such as, "What is the correct way to treat other human beings?" "Is it ever acceptable to intentionally hurt other people?" And, "Would I want someone treating me that way?" When people start asking these types of questions, a new level of consciousness has the ability to emerge. In fact, Thomas Jefferson once said, "Whenever you are to do a thing, though it can never be known but to yourself, ask yourself how you would act were all the world looking at you, and act accordingly."

We have an obligation to students to provide them with what they need to lead meaningful and productive lives. Many students have never critiqued their own way of thinking or behaving. Therefore, they have never had the opportunity to reflect on the meaning or the impact of their actions. As a result, they are more susceptible to do things that will harm or hurt themselves and others. This can be transformed with schools becoming intentional about including discussions on ethics and morality.

Current students can benefit from being exposed to conversations on ethics and morality. We have to be very clear that it no longer makes sense to teach a youngster to add, and neglect teaching him that stealing does not promote humanity. If we help to make someone intelligent and neglect to build his or her character, we have done them a disservice.

Because we live in an information age, students have immediate access to all types of information. Unfortunately, many students have not developed enough of an ethical and moral compass to accurately evaluate the information. Therefore, the information has the potential to promote harm just as much as it does wellness. For instance, any student today can learn from the internet how to construct a home-made bomb. Without adequate exposure to ethical and moral thinking and evaluation, this information can be used towards great destruction. Educators and other adults in children's lives must provide them with the opportunity to discuss , learn, evaluate, and decipher. Then we can witness better choices being made on a continuous basis.

I can recall one of the most beneficial classes I ever took in high school was 10th grade English. The reason was because the teacher, Mr. Donaldson, would often have the class discuss current events. Thus, in the 10th grade we would find ourselves discussing everything from pop culture to the latest geopolitical incident taking place in the world. As a class, we became thinkers, analyzers, and societal critics. Having that experience has convinced me that there is great benefit in asking young people to think critically and reflectively about the world in which they live, the problems they see, and how they want to make an impact. That is education at its finest. Young people engaged in thought on how to make the world a better place; learning ethics are important, morality matters, and character counts.

It is possible for young people to come to new ways of thinking about themselves and the world in which they live through discussion that

This is a time for concerned adults to be brave and push for some basic reforms in the educational system. There are a number of things to be done that would prove to be quite beneficial.

incorporates ethics and morality. The discussion can prompt new behavior that a student does on a daily basis. A student may decide after talking and thinking about it, that it is better to help someone with a disability than to make fun of them. Aristotle said, "Moral excellence comes about as a result of habit. We become just by doing just acts, temperate by doing temperate acts, brave by doing brave acts."

First, there needs to be a movement that empowers teachers and administrators to have control in the schools. No longer should any student be able to verbally or physically threaten and assault a teacher or administrator believing that nothing severe is going to happen to him/her. It must be clear that certain actions carry dire consequences. Also, no teacher or administrator should be made to feel they did something wrong by asserting themselves to maintain order within the school. If students think they can do anything without severe penalty, they will. If they think no one has the authority to stop their bad behavior, it will only escalate. Once they realize there is widespread support throughout the community for teachers and administrators to maintain order and civility, things can be different. If these changes were adopted and implemented, you would see entire schools transform in a relatively short time.

Secondly, there needs to be special attention paid to raising moral and ethical issues. One way to weave it into the life of the school can be by addressing it in the curriculum. If certain classes actually provided a context for moral and ethical dialogue, this would be a major benefit. There are currently printed materials that can be utilized for such courses. For instance, there is the Teaching Tolerance material that is produced by the Southern Poverty Law Center.(5) Any educator would find this material excellent for prompting thought-provoking conversations.

Thirdly, to further help students sort through the moral and ethical implications of their decisions, schools can bring in Rachel's Challenge. This is a non-profit organization that came into existence in memory of Rachel Scott, who was the first person killed in the Columbine High School massacre on that fateful day of April 20, 1999. Rachel's Challenge exists to inspire, equip and empower every person to create a permanent positive culture change in their school, business and community by starting a chain reaction of kindness and compassion. They also seek to create a safe learning environment for all students by re-establishing and delivering proactive antidotes to school violence and bullying. The organization sends out speakers who go to schools and share Rachel's incredible story. Students get to hear about the amazing way in which she lived her life, and then they are offered a very special challenge as the presentation concludes.

Finally, everyone can make the personal commitment to stay aware of what is happening in the educational institutions in their neighborhood. There may be various ways in which you can help them become more effective and more efficient. After all, we the people are the ones who allowed things to get like this, and we have the power to change and improve it. Also, we need to be knowledgeable of what is happening politically as it relates to education. We should not want to see schools incapable of improving because they lack the necessary resources.

If all of these things are implemented, schools around the nation can look and function differently. This is the time to take action. This is the time to get involved. This is the time to work for better days.

STOP! STOP! STOP!

What follows is *only* for
those who breathe..........

This is a <u>human alert</u> topic!
(You have the option to
skip to the next section.)

Behold...
The Only One Greater Than Yourself

"The time is always right to do what's right."
Dr. Martin Luther King, Jr.

Listen to the Wind
Education and Spirituality
by Lynnette Stallworth

Have you ever seen the wind? Not the effects of the wind. Not the leaves of a tree swaying. Not the clouds passing across the sky. Not a piece of paper tumbling through the street, but the cause of the movement. You know with certainty it, the wind is there. Where does it begin and where does it end? Have you ever seen the wind? You know the wind is there but you cannot see it.

Take a deep breath in. Hold it. Now slowly breathe out. Did you see your breath? You felt it move through your body for sure. You may even have heard the exhaling sound of your breath. This breathing happens constantly. Just as the wind is not seen neither is our breath. We feel even smell both but we do not see either.

These two forces ebb and flow. They are forms of energy. One resides outside of us and the other, breath resides within us. They are essential to sustaining life. They are life itself. For the most part we take it all for granted; in doing so we bypass the very presence of spirit. Spirit is our essence, energy invisible force for living. "Spiritus," the Latin origin of the word spirit means "breath." Long ago the philosopher DesCarte proposed, "...I think therefore I am..." African philosophy holds, '...I feel therefore I am...' How about "I breathe therefore I am." I am simultaneously fully human and spiritual. We are human beings, we are spiritual beings. We are beings both human and spiritual. If you breathe you are of spirit. Feel the wind? But it cannot be seen. Feel your breath? Yet it cannot be seen.

There is a moment during our formation in the womb when breathing begins. A mystery of life and conception that breath quickens – awakens a human into life. That breath installs an innate sacredness – a spirit. At our birth we are divine, sacred and spiritual.

In the video, My Spirituality as an Atheist, spirituality is fully claimed and embraced as the "essence of a human...uncommonly humbled and grateful...by awe of life itself."(6) The matter of humans being spiritual is not-not religious. Spirituality and religion are separate from one another – two different constructs. Spirit of an individual transcends their religion, faith, physical make-up, intellect or personality.

Everything has reason. There is form and function. And spirit too has purpose. Keep in mind while sacred spirit is forceful. In fact spirit is a paper incomparable to any other power. Spirit 'brings us to action and gives us ability from noticing beauty, feeling wonder and being in awe.' Spirit is the force that unleashes our imagination, creativity and striving for the other than.

The energy of spirit moves us to consider our actions. Spirit is energy that appears as kindness, forgiveness and hope! When you hear countless reports of heroic action or above and beyond sacrifice the question may be, "How did you do this or that?" or "What made you do this or that?"

The response most common is "... something just told me...," "there was nothing else to do...," "I had to..." this unseen force is as close as our breath yet beyond understanding gives power to do seemingly the impossible or improbable. The matter of spirit and spirituality is taken seriously in the legal profession. How many times has an attorney argued a case on the basis of *the spirit of law* rather than *the letter of the law*? There is even spiritual counseling available for police officers. A book entitled, *Spiritual Survival for Law Enforcement* is an indication

I.Q. and I.Q.

Consider this: Internal Quotient and Intelligence Quotient. When the two are distinguished a whole new perspective is created. Intelligence Quotient has long been a familiar measurement of human beings, but the human side alone is incomplete. What about the spirit; intangible, unseen; yet experienced by all? Here is an offering of an

Internal Quotient "I.Q." measurement and its effects.

of how the human spirit is becoming increasingly acknowledged and recognized.(7)

In the medical world time after time, families and loved ones are told "do whatever you can to keep spirits up," which suggests that spirit has an ability to add to the body's healing.

Along with other reasons for humans having a spirit it cannot be dismissed that spirit completes us. There is the obvious body. There is the ever explored mind. Our wholeness is rounded-off by spirit. Some are more comfortable thinking about and referring to spirit as emotions. Either way spirit is in need and worthy of acknowledgement, care and respect.

When there is true regard and recognition for spirit there are two possible tracks. There are outcomes when spirit is regarded, named as *hallow*; without regard for spirit the outcome is best named as *hollow*. As examples:

When Spirit is Regarded/ Held as hallow leads to:	When Spirit is **NOT** Regarded/ Held as hallow leads to:
• Enlivened • Bright • Receptive	• Dead • Dull • Closed
Peaceful, Harmonious, Prosperous World • Thriving, Respectful USA • Loving, Family • Successful, Education	Noisy, Wars, Destruction • Chaotic, Anger, Self-defeating • Home: Frantic, Overwhelmed, Anxious • School: Hectic, Dangerous, Stressful

America Right Now is:

• Technically advanced	• Chaotic, Anger, Self-defeating
	• Socially unjust
	• Spiritually wanting
	• Intellectually underachieving

Overall humans are erroneously relying only on the Intelligence Quotient (I.Q.), which measures on the basis of testing well. It's time in our evolution as humans to reconsider building our lives on "Internal Quotient" – I.Q. of the spirits standards such as creativity, non-violence, gratitude, kindness and happiness. After all we came into this life pure and fully equipped to live from the hallowed track. It is not oversimplifying to recommend that we chose the hallow track again. This current choice of hollowness is not working in our best interest. It's a good time to make a different choice.

It is imperative that education intentionally be infused with reverence for life, self, others; and be fully humane; body, mind and spirit and respectful to all creation.

It could be that we have forgotten our own sacredness. The darling four year old boy had just become a big brother. He went into the nursery to find his mother and newborn sister. The four year old asked if he could have private time with his sister. The mom being surprised and unsure said, "Okay, be gentle!" She placed the little sister in the big brothers arms and they settled safely and neatly on the loveseat. After what seemed like a long time she returned. The little boy returned his sister to their mom with a warm glow on his face. He turned as he walked to leave and said aloud, "I almost forgot I was perfect too!"

However it is done we need to remember we are still perfect expressions in spirit. Marianne Williamson's, *Return to Love,* is a refreshing, refilling and renewing reflection for remembering our true self.(8) Making the shift from hollow to hallowed brings clarity of purpose, improved relationships and less clutter within oneself.

"To Protect and Serve"

How education attends to the spirit of students will change the dynamic and results in the academic setting.

Before panic breaks out – this is not religion. This is filling a gap. This is including body, mind and spirit – the whole child in the educational endeavor. No more 'checking' the very essence of a child's humanness at the school drop-off.

"To Protect and Serve" is meant here is unlike law enforcement. "To Protect and Serve" for education is "protect" the *whole* child and "serve" the family. Every child deserves to be kept safe in body, mind and spirit. To protect from physical harm! To safeguard young minds with a full range of information; to respecting the spirit of a child and acknowledging is to protect it.

A child at every age or stage needs encouragement. To tell or suggest to a child they "cannot" become more is to inflict spiritual harm. To damage or attempt to kill a spirit is immoral. "To Protect and Serve" will ultimately benefit education itself. Honoring the wholeness of a child is a practice that supports the health of the family and can possibly break the current cycle of disconnect and dysfunction. The hopeful eventual outcome is excellence across the board in education for all students; and school and home functioning as MLK's "The Beloved Community."

None of us is perfect, but each of us is sacred.

Putting intentional efforts to celebrate and acknowledge the whole person – body, mind and spirit no doubt can and needs to take a variety of shapes.

Here are a few ideas:

Still time. This is not punishment. It is a directed quiet time. The purpose is to give time during a normally hectic day for the mind to catch up with the body and the spirit. We do tend to over-run ourselves. Each person will need to lie down in a comfortable position or put their head down, and lower the lights. No one moving or talking. Softly give a positive word to absorb; do for at least 10 minutes each day.

Listening to my life. Best in small group. Each person shares something they celebrate or are concerned about in their lives. No comment at all. Group response: "you have been heard." This exercise is meant to increase trust and learning that they are not alone, it is likely someone else has dealt with something similar.

Empowering time. May use picture board or storytelling. The objective is:
1. sharing a situation, using intuition to determine action, or no action;
2. build self-confidence to listen to themselves
3. develop mind, mouth and motion – think, speak, act.

Visualizing exercise. This exercise is simple and straightforward asking the class to close their eyes, quiet their minds and imagine themselves at their very best. The leader may then invite each to briefly describe their vision of their best self.

"I am" affirmation. Sitting or standing in a circle each person speaks robustly their personal "I am." Of course the more honest and positive the better. This is a powerful exercise for little ones up through adulthood.

Inspiring time. Possible to create this time in two ways. One is from Audre Lorde's saying "Who better to encourage me than myself?" Now that is a way to be in touch with one's own spirit as a permanent always available driving force. The other way to apply this time is from the "outside" asking "Who gives you great ideas?, Who or what encourages you?, What is your goal for this school year?" Of course the teacher/leader will know to adapt appropriately. Inspiring time is a diamond-in-the-rough, as it can assist putting together that which supports life-long success of drive and direction.

We often have one or the other. We have the energy, but don't have a clue what to do with it. Or we have ideas/goals, but not a drop of energy to move us forward. To have both at the same time is divine! It is matching will and understanding.

It's time to put our "Whole Self In" creating a combination quasi yoga and partial children's song "Hokey-Pokey" together embedded in the entire education system. We must make opportunities for body, mind and spirit to come together in great ways in order to produce phenomenal results.

As the charming children's book *Moo, Baa, La La La* by Sandra Boynton ends so does this writing, "It's quiet now what do you say?"(9) The possibilities are endless. Your desire and spirit's guidance will lead to a new day in education. Listen, *listen to the wind*.

The Largest Classroom in the School

An Interview with a Middle School Principal who desires anonymity
with Ushanda Pauling

Please give us a little bit of your background. How many years have you been in education?

I have been an educator for 12 years. My current position is principal of a middle school, grade levels 6-8 in an urban setting.

What is the importance of education as you see it?

Considering that today's children are our current future, the importance of education is paramount! Education affords us the opportunity to broaden our horizons and experience things that may not be afforded to us in other settings. A solid education is important because it has the propensity to open doors that would otherwise be closed for students.

Exposure on field trips and technological opportunities are also very important to education. Yes, schools and educators are charged with EDUCATING our students, but it's also a moral imperative we provide other opportunities for exposure. Many of these areas of exposure are provided through external classroom experiences. For instance, if an eighth grade U.S. History teacher in Jacksonville, FL is teaching a unit on slavery, it would be no more than appropriate to visit Kingsley Plantation located just 15 miles outside of Jacksonville. Extensions of lessons via technological experiences and field trips are paramount. While visiting a science class last school year, I observed the "light bulb" come on when a teacher used active technology to explain how neurons affect thinking, movement and other brain functions. Units, standards, and benchmarks can all be brought to life through these ancillary type experiences.

Would you share some of your thoughts about our current education system?

Our current education system is in a time of great change. Recognizing we are truly in the age of accountability, professional educators can no longer teach the way they have taught in the past. Post-secondary opportunities for students are now requiring "all" individuals come prepared in ways our forefathers never would have imagined. Therefore, our current education system demands teachers teach differently because demands on students are higher and opportunities for post-secondary experiences are more demanding.

Teachers cannot work in isolation. They must plan together and be aware of ever-changing student data. Instruction must be differentiated to meet the needs of all students. Recognizing all students don't learn the same way on the same day, it's imperative that differentiation of instruction is evident in ALL classrooms. At times differentiated instruction may look and sound chaotic, but has proven to be best for students. Data driven grouping of students, use of ancillaries, and use of stations are some examples of differentiated instruction.

In your opinion, how do schools benefit parents?

Schools benefit parents in many ways. Many schools and districts are committed to on-going parent involvement. Family Involvement Centers have become a very popular way to engage parents while teaching them skills that can assist in their parenting. Parents have the opportunity to get to know what's going on with their child, support the school and have more input/voice regarding choices being made at the school level.

What is the trick to being successful in school?

The trick to being successful in school is to "never give up!" At times things become very difficult in school. However, it's imperative that students never give up in their quest for academic proficiency.

Complete this thought please, "At school children learn...?"

How to communicate with others, receive constructive criticism, and identify the learning style that works best for them and to deal with varying personalities.

These skills are taught through use of daily classroom experiences. Classroom teachers are trained to provide students with valuable experiences that will ultimately assist in their overall academic success and personal growth.

What do state standardized tests say about the education of students?

Standardized tests are merely a "snap shot" of what a student may know. I agree with the fact that a form of accountability should be in place, however, I have difficulty placing a students' overall success on one test. A student's level of educational success should not only be based on standardized tests, but also on their daily level of proficiency in classroom experiences.

What ways can parents get more "involved" in schools?

Parents can get more involved in schools, by visiting their children's school (announced and unannounced), become an active part in the local Parent Teacher Student Association (PTSA), supporting various school related events, and ensuring students are completing homework and other school assignments.

How could the education system be completely overhauled?

When you find out, let me know!!!!!!

Have you ever been "schooled" by a student?

Students have "schooled" me both in and out of the classroom. As a classroom teacher, I had students to "check" me and quickly let me know that there was more than one way to solve a problem and come to a resolution regarding an academic issue.

I can tell a story...

On a fairly regular basis we have students acting out and not fully engaged in class. There was an especially difficult seventh grader, "*Floyd*," that gave one of my teachers a run for her money. This teacher spent most of the year really disliking this young man. He was angry, acted out, and consistently in trouble. He really never seemed to feel a sense of belonging in the school community. This one particular teacher could not break through with this young man; she was consistently frustrated, and often sent him out of the classroom. Other teachers and administrators in the school didn't really know this young man, he came later in the school year from a different area and we just hadn't connected with him.

One weekend she attended an art show for the local Department of Children and Families. In the corridors of the art exhibit there were pictures lining the walls. The pictures showed the faces and first names of boys and girls awaiting adoptive families. As she continued down the hall, she suddenly came upon a photo of our seventh grader Floyd. She was instantly dumbfounded, convicted by her bad feelings and dislike for Floyd. After some questioning she discovered that Floyd had been waiting to be adopted for several years and had been bouncing around from place to place. She was so upset by his situation.

She requested to speak at our next faculty meeting. The realization of his turbulent childhood had a very profound impact on her. She had been so moved by Floyd's situation. She felt that she had done such a disservice to Floyd over the course of the school year that she wanted to warn other teachers and administrators to take heed. In all the times that she scolded, disciplined, and dismissed Floyd she had never taken the time to get to know him. He wasn't asked about his background or behavior. She was not the only one, several of us failed him. She spoke during the faculty meeting about the importance of making the time to get to know our students and to take an interest in their lives, considering that each student comes with a story. She noted that it is critical to meet each student where they are to engage them in the learning process.

This was a glaring example for me of students "schooling" us. So many of us carry on from day to day and don't bother to consider that there may be a little bit more under the behaviors of our students. I can tell you, this teachers perspective took a total change and she has made it part of her day to get to know students well beyond their names.

Let's go back to possible ways to overhaul the current school system. What are a few ways that come to your mind that might be helpful to making change?

How about my top 5 things to change? I'll just list them because they pretty much speak for themselves.

1. Mandate Head Start Programs.
2. Standardized testing should be reflective of where students begin/end.
3. Better selection of elective classes.
4. Classroom teaching should be more transparent.
5. Re-address the true of fidelity of the mission associated with various magnet schools.

It is My Considered View as a School Board Member

by April Griffin

I believe most people want our children to be successful; we all just have a different idea of how to make that happen. We know if our children are successful, our society will be successful. What this looks like to me from a very elementary level is that more people will be employed and paying into a tax base, thereby less people will be in need of government services. In the long run when our children win, we all win.

Thomas Jefferson, who was one of the first Americans to talk about creating a public education system, felt education should be available to all people, irrespective of their status in society. He knew a sound government could only exist with an educated citizenry, as evidenced in his quote "whenever the people are well-informed, they can be trusted with their own government; that, whenever things get so far wrong as to attract their notice, they may be relied on to set them right." As hard as Jefferson tried he could not separate education from government.

People often ask why I ran for public office; school board in particular, especially considering that in the political arena, the school board is considered pretty low on the totem pole. Most people do not realize that school districts are typically the largest employer in a community, accounts for the largest portion of the state's budget, and that school taxes are one of the largest line items on a property tax bill; yet the position for school board is typically at the bottom of the ballot. It is also one of the hardest political offices to raise money for. And unlike most every other elected official, school board members don't have dedicated staff to support them in doing research, attending community events, or responding to constituent needs. In large school districts, lack of support can sometimes make the job overwhelming. All of this being said, I love my job! Being a school board member is one of the most thankless and at the same time rewarding jobs, and I am doing satisfying work. So to answer the question "I want to make a difference in children's lives, I want to speak for children who don't have a voice and I want to help children who are getting lost in the system."

I strongly agree with the former U.S. Speaker of the House Tip O'Neil who said, "All politics is local." So after more than a decade of working to elect many other people and having a lot of people encourage me to run for office; I decided school board was the perfect fit for me. I also knew not being carved from the mold of a typical school board member would allow me to bring a unique perspective and much needed voice to the school district. As a child I not only failed out of the public school system, the public school system failed me. I believe a lot can be learned from failure.

Over time I have come to believe that political agendas and big business are the two main driving forces behind most of the major decisions made by educational and political leaders. I remember the day I came to the realization of "who was schooling who." I had only been a school board member for a few months when I experienced my "aha" moment. Shortly after I was elected, I was told by most of the veteran school board members I served with that I needed to attend a bi-annual conference of school board members, school superintendents, and school board attorneys. This conference was very well attended by school district decision makers from across the state. There were a lot of very informative sessions throughout the day. I learned about school finance, school law, and current legislative issues affecting public schools.

At the end of the first day, attendees were treated to a reception sponsored by various educational vendors. As I walked into that huge tent on that first night, I was a bit overwhelmed by its opulence. Nice events were not new to me; as I have attended and planned many different functions and events in my lifetime, from weddings, Bar/ Bat Mitzvahs, charity events, and Gasparilla Balls. So, it was clear to me this function cost a pretty penny. I knew education was a big business when I ran for office, but I was pretty naïve as to how big it was. In that moment standing in the entrance of that grand tent, I realized what was driving education decisions, at least in large part. With my basic knowledge of marketing, I knew big dollars were, at stake for these vendors to spend the kind of resources they were to essentially advertise their products and/or services. There is a lot of money to be made from public education and I have kept this night in mind as I serve. There are a lot of jobs to be given to family members and friends and contracts, etc. to be gained in the public education arena. Fortunately I don't have a horse in either of those races, so I can serve as if I have nothing to lose. I am constantly reminding myself of why I ran for the school board in the first place.

As I provide my perspective on public education I will reference Florida; Hillsborough County in particular, not only because this is my frame of reference, but also because Hillsborough County is a microcosm of the United States. There is a very diverse population in this community. Consider Hillsborough Counties' multi-generational immigrants and first generation immigrants, its' urban and suburban areas, its' diverse post-secondary educational community with everything ranging from public universities and community colleges to private universities and many options for career and technical education, and last but not least, the rich, historic agriculture of this community. Hillsborough County is essentially a demographic snap shot of America.

It is important to keep in mind that along with a diverse population there are diverse issues. Issues that have to be addressed in each community residing within its boundaries or we cannot expect to live in a safe and vibrant area. A significant issue we need to deal with is challenging our students to achieve their highest potential, while responding to the business community to ensure we are graduating students with the skills they require to be successful in an ever-changing world.

Let's first examine the current financial climate in public education. A lot of public resources are geared towards a very small percentage of our students. Unfortunately low graduation rates, especially among financially disadvantaged and minority students, have been shrouded for far too long by inaccurate data and reporting and the fact there is no national standard to accurately determine graduation rates. But by digging deeper into the data and doing some very rudimentary math we can see that nationally, one-third of students—about 1.3 million each year—leave high school without a diploma, according to the Alliance for Excellent Education. (10) In other words, 67 percent of students leave high school with a diploma. According to the U.S. Bureau of Labor Statistics, of that 67 percent of high school graduates, 70.1 percent were enrolled in colleges or universities in 2009, and of the 70.1 percent of high school graduates who were enrolled in college in 2009 the US News World Report estimates that 30 percent of college and university students drop out after their first year and 50 percent never graduate. (11)

Let me add one more thing to consider, although I was not able to find any sound data on how many college graduates are working outside of their chosen degree, anecdotally I know a lot of people who do not use their degrees in their current jobs.

So what does all of this mean? Let's do that rudimentary math now. Using 100 students as the baseline and the data above: if out of 100 students, 67 percent will graduate with a high school diploma, and 70 percent (which is approximately 47 students) enroll in college, of those 47 students only 50 percent graduate, that means only 24 out of 100 students will graduate college with a degree. Add to that equation the number of graduates who are not even working in their chosen degree field and someone can easily see we are spending the bulk of our resources on making every student college bound and losing sight of the majority of our students. I believe we are doing a disservice; not only to our students, but our society as a whole.

We must be willing to accept that not every child is going to college and admit that it is all right to have students go into a post secondary educational scenario that will teach them a skill set to lead to a highly productive career. We must also be willing to accept they may graduate high school and go straight into the workforce. Who is to say these same students will not return to school in the future to increase their opportunity for growth and success within their chosen career path? I had a college professor once say the best decision she ever made was to drop out of college when she was nineteen years old, and the second best decision she ever made was to go back later in life. Data proves most young adults do not seem to be ready for college right out of high school.

In the basic formula above I did not complicate matters by breaking those 100 students down using subgroups like poverty, learning disabilities, gender, language barriers, or race. But I want to give a ten thousand foot overview of some of these dynamics, because the reality is that there are some very regrettable issues that have to be factored into the equation every day due to the sub-groups. Some of these issues we have to contend with are higher than normal drop-out rates, gang activity, high incarceration rates, teen pregnancy, sexually transmitted diseases (STDs), and homelessness, just to name a few. I want to put a statistic on at least one of these factors so it is clear how our society can no longer afford to fail any of our students. According to research conducted by the Council of Great City Schools—in 2008, black males were twice as likely to drop out of high school as white males. (12) There are going to be successes and failures, but for the sake of the greater good of our community we need to be willing and able to address each one is presented to us in a realistic and productive way.

Our economy has also presented some variables into the equation. For example, universities, just like everyone else, are trying to figure out how they are going to survive. They see students as revenue generating units (RGU) who are part of the new business plan created to ensure their survival. Because of this new school of thought there is a massive push geared towards making every child who walks the halls of public education "college bound". I doubt there are many people who would argue against the statement that obtaining a college degree could set someone up for a more financially productive career. But truly analyzing data tells us that having a degree does not necessarily guarantee anything but an enormous amount of debt incurred from student loans.

Consider this; total student borrowing more than doubled nationwide in the past decade, to $86 billion, according to the College Board and the private loan portion spiked sevenfold. About two-thirds of students graduate with debt, which on average has more than doubled since 1993 to about $20,000. And the number with at least $40,000 in debt has increased tenfold in the same period, to more than 70,000, according to the Project on Student Debt. (13)

A study by CNN Money analyst Jessica Dickler reports in 2008 "There was a record number of unemployed college graduates seeking work. So many, in fact, they outnumber high school dropouts on the job hunt" and "In November the number of people with a higher degree who were out of work rose to 1.413 million from 1.411 million in the previous month, according to the Bureau of Labor Statistics. Comparatively, there were 1.282 million unemployed high school dropouts, up slightly from 1.273 million in October." (14)

Neal McCluskey, an education analyst at the Cato Institute, a think tank in

Washington, feels the number of college graduates who are unemployed sends a clear message that college degrees do not necessarily make someone more employable or increase their ability to earn higher wages. He says "the majority of people who are going to college today are really just getting a piece of paper," and "the bottom line is we always insist everybody has to go to college without in any way discriminating or determining whether actually going to college is providing the skills to make one more employable. All that matters, especially to the politicians, is that everybody is getting a piece of paper -- a college degree." This brings me back to my contention that colleges are struggling for their own survival and see each person enrolled as a revenue generating unit (RGU). I have spoken to professors who are very frustrated with this new philosophy and are having a crisis of faith that they are not really helping people better themselves, but just "getting them across the stage to earn a piece of paper to hang on their wall."

There are many successful graduates of the public school system who have gone on to great careers; with or without college, and have become productive members of society. We must embrace these successes, but we cannot lose sight of the high dropout rate in our nation. We need to be proud of, and hold up our successes, but we cannot continue to just throw money hand over fist at public education without really using true data to make our decisions.

Educators in the public sector are being forced to go in too many different directions. Accountability, data, college readiness, choice, high stakes testing, and standardization are the current buzz words being thrown around by politicians and educators alike. There are some very valid arguments for each of these concepts, but we must look deeper and follow the money trail. Remember what I said about public education being one of the largest line items on a property tax bill and accounting for over half of the state of Florida's budget?

We all bring our experiences to the table when making decisions. I have brought my experiences to my position as a school board member and I believe Dr. Eric J. Smith, who is currently Florida's Commissioner of Education is using his experience when making choices for Florida's students. Prior to this appointment to Florida's Commissioner of Education he was employed by the College Board, as the Senior Vice President of College Readiness. The goal of making every child ready for college is an admirable and lofty goal and I am in no way implying there is anything other than life experience and a belief that college is the best path to success. Under Dr. Smith's leadership, more College Board programs have been pushed from the top down in public schools. And let's face it, most educators own path to success was college.

While wanting to make sure every child has the skills necessary to be successful in college is a commendable goal, we cannot have a cookie cutter approach to educating our children. Each child is unique and the needs of our communities are unique. We will always have a need for plumbers, electricians, auto mechanics, hospitality workers, first responders, and other careers that may only need a certification, not a degree.

Let me give a real life example of how we are trying to make education one size fit all. One day I was taking a tour with the Hillsborough County Farm Bureau and met a very intelligent, articulate young man. He was a senior in high school; was voluntarily taking two advance placement (AP) classes, raising an animal for show, and had a part time job. He was originally scheduled for three advance placement classes, but he only wanted two. With all his busy and very commendable schedule held, he felt he was only capable of maintaining two AP classes. Following the proper chain of command he asked his guidance counselor to remove one of the classes from his schedule and replace it with an agriculture class but was told he needed the extra AP class if he was going to apply to the University of Florida(UF). He told her that he already spoken to admissions at UF and had taken enough AP classes. Eventually he was taken out of the third AP class only to subsequently be put right back in. He met with the guidance counselor a second time. Informed her about the mix up and requested it be fixed. Again, he was taken out of the class and put in an agriculture class, and again his schedule changed putting him back in the third AP class. He eventually met with the principal and expressed his concerns and the situation was resolved. Think about this. This young man had the wherewithal and the fortitude to respectfully advocate for his cause. How many young adults are taught this type of communication at home and won't just capitulate to the powers that be? Or how many would share their concerns with authority in a disrespectful or unproductive way? We know that either of these scenarios would most likely yield negative results.

I hear about situations like this all the time from students, parents, teachers, and even guidance counselors. This directive is from higher up the chain than anyone at the school site level. But no one is going to fight it for fear they might harm their own careers.

I know we can accomplish things others can't even imagine and I want to be a part of that effort. It is now my job to figure out how to help all children achieve their full potential in a political and financial climate that doesn't seem to want to create success for all children. Regardless of what questions are being asked, and by whom; there is one thing that is for certain, politicians and businesses do not need to map out the road to success for our children.

It is important when speaking about what needs to be done to reform public education we include all shareholders. We need to include students, parents, teachers, people from the business community, and not just chambers, but small business owners, government agencies, unions, and civic leaders, etc. Way too often school districts only engage chambers and chamber types at the head of the table when making decisions. Small business owners are hiring public school graduates too.

Public education is facing historic challenges. Maybe history will describe these years on par with the founding of our public education system and Brown v. Board. Who knows? The decisions currently being made and the decisions that will be made over the next decade, will decide whether our public education system should be completely dismantled and privatized or if we just adapt our current system to account for a global economy and new generations of students who learn completely different from the generations before them.

Based on my research and many conversations with educators, parents, students, leaders in higher education, and the people who hire the students who graduate from public school, I have found most people; including myself, agree education reform in the public sector is necessary. From everything I have learned, we need to adapt to the world around us if we are going to compete with it. We can't be apathetic and continue to make the same mistakes. I am reminded of Albert Einstein's often used quote "insanity is doing the same thing over and over again and expecting different results." But we can't completely dismantle public education and start from scratch, as is being proposed by Florida's current Governor, Rick Scott.

How are we going to make our public education system better if we don't address the problems head on and come up with some creative changes? Until we truly address the problems, hearing the voices of educators, students, parents, and community leaders, we will continue to make the same mistakes. We have the potential to be amazing. Our forefathers knew this. We are in a time of great change and in the words of one of our greatest founding fathers Thomas Jefferson, "Whenever the people are well-informed, they can be trusted with their own government." This then applies to the challenge before us all to transform America's educational system.

I invite you to become more informed and then find your place to be the needed change.

SEMESTER III

Assembly

Education is a right not a privilege; at least that is what we are told as Americans. However, a *good* education in America has become a *privilege* and not a *right*. That is what several parents have come to realize when they try to put their children in better public schools in a different district in the same city. Some parents have been arrested and charged with stealing funds in addition to being fined and forced to repay the difference owed in taxes.

Such was the case in January 2011 with a homeless mother, Tanya McDowell, in Bridgeport, Connecticut. Ms. McDowell used the address of her babysitter in Norwalk, Connecticut to place her five year old son in kindergarten. As a result of this situation, McDowell was charged with a felony for theft of over $15,000 and she faces up to 20 years in prison. (15)

A similar case occurred around the same time, January 2011 in Akron, Ohio. Kelley Williams-Bolar, a single mother in subsidized housing, was jailed for 9 days for sending her two daughters to a high school in suburban Copley-Fairlawn district. The single mother used their father's address to claim residency status so that her daughters could attend the better school. Ms. Williams-Bolar received fines of $30,000 for the cost of tuition and $6,000 for investigative cost.(16) Both cases are being appealed.

The unfortunate matter here is the disparity in funds that are distributed among public schools. Why would one public school have better accommodations and educational advances than another public school in the same city? Why would the school district in any city or state allow this to be the standard without someone stopping to ask, "Is this fair?" Does one set of students deserve a better education than other students?

Why are funds so disproportionately distributed? What is the formula used when funds are dispersed among public schools and who decides that it is correct? These are possibly the questions the arrested and jailed parents were asking when they decided to make sure their child received the same quality education as other students in the city. These are similar questions asked during segregation when black schools received fewer funds than white schools in the same city. Have we decided to revisit this era in a different way by saying one district deserves a better education than others?

Some reasons given for the disparity in funds is parents who live in more affluent areas pay more taxes than parents in less affluent areas and therefore deserve to have better funding in their schools. Who is to say the funds from the less affluent areas are not being used to make the schools in the more affluent areas better? This could be the reason why some of the parents who were arrested decided to place their child in a better equipped school. They wanted to make sure they received their monies worth for the taxes they were paying.

All parents want the best for their child(ren) no matter what area of town they choose or can afford to live in. As Americans, we should want the best for all citizens and not display an "us against them" mentality so that a good education will be a right for all who want one.

by Veronica Blakely

"What Had Happened Was..."

Ushanda Pauling with contribution by Deirdra Paulk

What had happened was...; a phrase used to sidestep 'the whole truth and nothing but the truth.' If and when someone says, "What had happened was...," know that a tale is about to be spun. The listener is being, to one degree or another, informed and/or misled for the purpose of evasion.

For example, a $20 bill is given to buy one loaf of bread for $2.79, one dozen medium eggs for $1.67 and one quart of milk for $2.96, totaling $7.42. However, $5.62 change is given back from the $20 bill. When you inquire about what happened to the rest of your change and the response is, "Well, what had happened was...," buckle up and get ready to be taken on an unforgettable ride.

Have you ever thought about what exactly happens to the almighty dollar once it is distributed to the local school districts? Have you ever wondered how some schools appear to have more than others? These are some piercing questions especially if you have ever had the opportunity to get a glimpse of what the inconsistencies are from state-to-state, county-to-county, city-to-city, and lastly school-to-school.

I have resided in three other states and found the health of a school district is based upon the focus of the tax payers and the school boards once the money has been distributed. Some school districts were proactive meaning they knew children were coming, and built land for a school. And put a clause in the home builders contracts that if they build homes they must designate land for a school." Another school district was home grown; it was a small town and didn't operate on a "county" system. For the most part the wealth was evenly distributed, and financial equality showed throughout. Yet, other counties, including in and around our nation's capital, were deemed some of the worst public school systems in the country. For those who can afford to send their children to private schools they do but there were constant reports of the public schools being dilapidated and there was lack of funding to adequately educate students.

It appears that education is scrutinized with a fine-tooth comb or with a high-powered magnifying glass. The federal government and state governments have formulas that take into consideration the wealth of the state, county, city and its population before funding is appropriated. One would think this would constitute a fair distribution of government monies to support education. So how can there be so many inconsistencies?

The following information will focus primarily on the "Sunshine State" Florida. Here is my local school districts' annual budget process: pulled from the *Financial Handbook Budget/Hillsborough County Public Schools*

Annual School Budget = Board approved rates (provided w/ principal's packet) x projected student count.

Art & Science Supplies Budget = # students in course master x board approved rates.

Career and Technical Supply Funds - prepared by career and technical division.(17)

Budgets are used at the Principal's discretion. Budgets are allocated no later than May 1st. Budgets may be transferred immediately after allocation. Requisitions may be processed – dated for delivery July 1 or after. Budgets increase after 5th month January - if student count increases 5% or more. Year-end financial calendar provided in March with specific budget deadline dates. This snapshot will help with your calculations.

Any reasonable person looking to become involved or even stimulate their own awareness would be lost in the first two lines of this calculation. How do we investigate what is happening with dollars in education? When legislation makes decisions or we are asked to elect public officials and trust those in educational decision making seats; how do we know they will understand this or even calculate in such a way that is transparent, fair, and equitable for all students?

According to the Florida Department of Education's website, the formula looks like this:

Distributing State Dollars

Overview – The amount of GROSS STATE AND LOCAL FLORIDA EDUCATION FINANCE PROGRAM (FEFP) DOLLARS for each school district is determined in the following manner:

WEIGHTED FULL-TIME EQUIVALENT (FTE) STUDENTS =
FTE Students × Program Cost Factors

BASE FUNDING =
Weighted FTE Students × Base Student Allocation (BSA)
× District Cost Differential (DCD)

GROSS STATE AND LOCAL FEFP DOLLARS =
Base Funding + DJJ Supplement + Declining Enrollment Supplement + Sparsity Supplement + Discretionary Contribution + 0.748 Mills Discretionary Compression + 0.25 Mills Additional Discretionary Compression + Safe Schools + Reading Program + Supplemental Academic Instruction + ESE Guaranteed Allocation + Merit Award Program (MAP) Allocation + Instructional Materials + Teachers Lead + Student Transportation + State Fiscal Stabilization Funds (SFSF) Allocation + Minimum Guarantee. (18)

In 1973 the Florida Legislature enacted the Florida Education Finance Program (FEFP). This act established the state's policy for equalizing funding to guarantee each student in the Florida public education system the availability of programs and services appropriate to his or her educational needs that are substantially equal to those available to any similar student notwithstanding geographic differences and varying local economic factors. The primary source of the funding comes from sales tax and, to a lesser degree, property taxes.

In technical terms, the Florida Department of Education exists to provide equalization of educational opportunity. The FEFP formula recognizes: (1) varying local property tax bases; (2) varying education program costs; (3) varying costs of living; and (4) varying costs for equivalent educational programs due to scarcity and dispersion of the student population. A key feature of the FEFP is that it bases financial support for education upon the individual student participating in a particular educational program rather than upon the number of teachers or classrooms.

The FEFP is the foundation for funding the public school system in Florida's K-12 education programs. However, there are other sources that will be addressed later in this chapter. There are many factors considered in the delegation of funds. The calculations for allocating finances are based on a full-time equivalent (FTE) student. This student has membership in one or more FEFP programs for a school year or its equivalent. For purposes of calculating the full-time equivalent student membership, a student is considered in membership until he or she withdraws or until the eleventh consecutive school day of his or her absence. The total report is 42 pages long and twists and turns readers through various facts and figures to calculate how each school receives its funding. Some say there is no parent support and community buy in; who can keep up with this? Programs, adjustments, funds, allocations, supplements, discretionary compression; a parent or community member would need a separate concordance just to translate the terminology in to readable words. These figures go through six calculations before a final number is determined. If you have a free week to read through all of the pages and calculations and special exceptions, it could be an interesting read.(18)

As an exceptional student education teacher within the public school system, I have learned the importance of the accuracy needed in reporting the services that are being rendered to all levels of FTE students. For example, if the student is receiving "X" number of hours of Special Education services, there is an amount that is designated for the student, but if it is not accurately reported, the district can miss out on collecting monies.

The 10-day student head count is another vital school funded source. The first 10 days of a new school year equates to dollars- Florida's base student rate = $3,623.76 per student. Additional funds are attached through add-ons for Special Education and English Speakers of Other Languages (ESOL). The exact amount is based on the individual student's matrix of services they are set to receive. Individual school budgets have some flexibility in spending based on the principal's discretion. This opens the door for *creative accounting* and sometimes strong-arm tactics for students who may be on the cusp academically or behaviorally.

Government assistance is available for students in Special Education classes. However, in some communities this assistance is known as a *"crazy check."* While the term is socially unacceptable and certainly not politically correct, there is an understanding about the crazy check. To define it in social terms, the crazy check is sought out by parents and sometimes school personnel to put a student into special education classes and on a track to receive a 12th grade certificate of completion instead of a traditional high school diploma. The crazy check is financial compensation that the student's family receives on a monthly basis. Professionals in the field of psychological testing report that students are tested (by schools and/or medical professionals) and information is collected from the family to support a diagnosis or recommendations for the student's need to be in Special Education. The financial benefit has become very attractive to families in some communities in financial hardship as a form of income. Even so, there are several variables that really impact a parent's decision to accept the diagnosis, educational track, future possibilities, and limitations for the student on top of the temporary financial gain and long term financial limits. The manipulative side of this assistance typically plays out like this:

1. Student is a regular behavioral challenge; disciplined often.
2. Student may have some learning deficiencies or needs additional help.
3. Family is typically (but not always) not well-educated and generally living in poverty or low income neighborhood.
4. Student is tested by school psychologist or referred for counseling to school social worker.
5. Parent is presented with:
   - Child's behavior and constant disruption reports from teachers;
   - Test results if already conducted (or strongly encouraged to authorize testing);
   - Strong encouragement to change the child's educational track (which can be where the future implications of the certificate of completion are glossed over);
   - A potential financial benefit to support the child throughout their primary education; and
   - Potential access to other community benefits while the student is in school and once they complete school.

An immediate thought might be, "Why doesn't the parent just say no or look into the implications of this further?" Remember, typically this occurs in low income areas among undereducated people, so the need for the financial benefit may be very attractive. It can become a way to keep the child in the school system and avoid them being kicked out because of bad behavior, or the guardian's lack of education intimidates them from digging in to the matter more and seemingly appearing in opposition of the authority figures at the school.

We present this to you as another spoke in the financial wheel of education. While families might receive a financial benefit, schools are also able to cash in on the increased amount given by the state to support the education and supplemental services for these students. You may shutter at the thought of anyone purposefully misusing this funding on the school's end or on the family's end, but it is a sad reality. All, of course, do not engage in this practice, and Special Education is valuable; this is given as something else to consider about the financing of education.

In addition to the base student rate and the additional ESOL and special education allotments per student, each school has their own operating budget for the school year. This is set by the board based on a number of variables. There are minimums in certain accounts that can be used in the designated areas. For accountability sake, as long as the rationale for the expense appears to be used for the intended purpose or a closely affiliated one, it can pass.

There are other resources, such as Title I funds that do not have the same flexibility to move and shift around; they must be used for the proposed purpose. Colleagues of mine serve as contract providers in school districts across the country. One shared a time where he was talking with a school about contracting services for a pull out group of students. The school administrator was really interested in the programming but that particular line item in the budget didn't have enough available funds. The administrator suggested they would pull from another line item to cover the costs and needed my colleague to invoice separately to allow payment to come from different sources to cover the program. For example, invoice for materials to pull from a supplies budget, invoice for contracted hours to come from Title I funding, and invoice other expenses to come from another line item to collectively make up the total program implementation cost.

Just to show how intricate this is, here is a sample of the Hillsborough County annual school budget allocation process:

A. School Supplies Budget will be sent early May.

B. A worksheet showing the available line items with a space for the amount will be included.

C. We recommend that at least 10% be put into contingency – for a potential reduction in 20th day student count.

D. Budget for teaching supplies may be allocated by department, teacher, or any other method allocation that works for your school.

E. Budget for art & science supplies should be allocated in projects 7001 & 7002 for tracking purposes.

F. Projects 7003-7997 may be used to further separate budget by department or teacher.

G. We recommend that budget dollars be placed into a classroom supply account specifically for the purchase of paper for all staff.

H. Other line items that must be budgeted are postage, office supplies and custodial supplies.

I. A line item often overlooked is custodial gasoline for mowers and other lawn equipment.

J. Prepare a budget transfer to spread or allocate your budget.

K. You will be notified of any adjustments for 20th day or 5th month Student Count – budget placed in contingency.

L. Each line item or account should be reconciled monthly against your Cost Center Report. (17)

Who Else Funds Education?

School Districts also receive outside funding from lotteries, gambling casinos, and race track funds. This is another source of income for the education system which includes both K-12th grades as well as secondary education. The pie chart shows the dollar amounts that are distributed to each sector of education based on the monies generated from the sale of lottery tickets. The lottery has been a blessing to my family because of the Bright Futures Scholarship. My oldest daughter applied, met the criteria and was awarded a scholarship for the entire four years of college as long as she maintained the requirements. At the college level, this is definitely a wonderful scholarship. This allows the students to have access to a free or subsidized education for average to above average performing students. Tracking the use of the money is simple. As a matter of fact, all the pieces of the pie chart seem to have a clear road to how the funds are utilized with the exception of the public school piece.

Property taxes, Students with Disabilities programs, private contributions, federal government (in the form of The American Recovery and Reinvestment Act), The Education Jobs Fund, Race to the Top Grant Program are all financial sources that fluctuate in their support of public education.

Think specifically about the property tax factor for a minute. Most, if not all states and commonwealths apportion a percentage from property taxes specifically to underwrite budgeted education. The property tax for education has long been *not enough*. Other funding sources have been created over the years to pay for education like lotteries and casinos. Despite multiple sources specifically designated to fully fund education, it continues to be *not enough*.

Given the declined economy, particularly the depressed housing market, foreclosures, and decreased housing values, the collection of property taxes have placed an even more severe deficiency in the funding for public education. There is now really not enough, in fact, education is now in the position to have to give back.

Let's take a look at some examples of lotteries at work to fund education.

Dollars to Education
MORE THAN $22 BILLION TO EDUCATION!

The Florida Lottery's mission is to maximize revenues for the enhancement of public education in Florida. With this focus, the Florida Lottery has not only kept its promise as a committed partner in education, but has also operated as a distinguished and outstanding business enterprise.

In fiscal year 2009-2010, the Florida Lottery transferred more than $1.24 billion to the Educational Enhancement Trust Fund. For the eighth time in the Florida Lottery's 23-year history, the agency surpassed the billion-dollar mark in a single year. The Lottery's total contribution since start-up is more than $22 billion. Although this contribution is only a small part of the state's overall education budget, the impact of the Florida Lottery on public education flows from community to community.

Educational Enhancement Trust Fund Appropriations

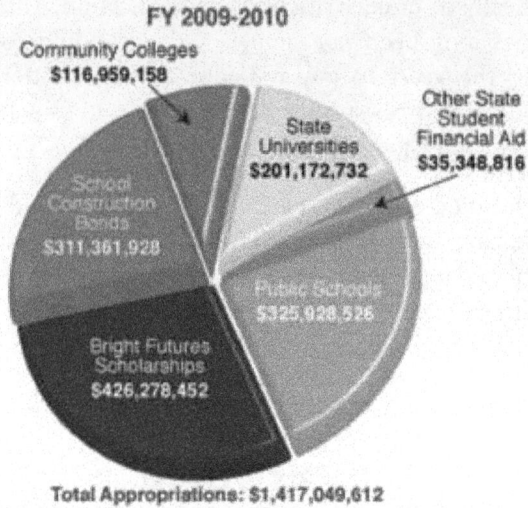

FY 2009-2010

Community Colleges
$116,959,158

Other State
Student
Financial Aid
$35,348,816

State
Universities
$201,172,732

School
Construction
Bonds
$311,361,928

Public Schools
$325,928,526

Bright Futures
Scholarships
$426,278,452

Total Appropriations: $1,417,049,612

*Education appropriations from Lottery sales are based on the Revenue Estimating Conference's projections for the year. Lottery funds are appropriated by the Florida Legislature and administered by the Florida Department of Education. Revenue sources for the Educational Enhancement Trust Fund include net proceeds of lottery games (approximately 90%) and slot machine revenue tax (approximately 10%). (19)

One school reports they received lottery funding one year (2008), and for the last two years they have received NO lottery funding. When you look at the billboards along the side of major roads and highways noting that X amount of dollars have gone to education and that schools receive real dollars to fund education, something seems off. So who determines what schools and how much?

County Contributions

If you ever have the time or interest; visit your state lottery website to see county by county distribution of funds. This is a quick comparison of my local county school district and a Missouri county.

HILLSBOROUGH County Florida	
Year	K-12 Grade
2007-08	$29,406,910
2008-09	$23,813,883
2009-10	$23,179,523
Total	**$590,087,449**
Bright Futures College Scholarships	**$247,752,857**
Funding for School Construction	**$328,119,408***
TOTAL EDUCATION FUNDING	**$1,817,926,961** (19)

CARROLL County, Missouri	
Year	K-12 Grade
2007-08	$579,917
2008-09	$157,693
2009-10	$196,103
Total	**$933,713** (20)

It appears that one of the reasons, as a substitute teacher, I saw differences in individual's school technology and "wealth" of the school is because principals have the flexibility to allocate money to specific causes within their schools. Depending on the philosophy of the principal is where emphasis is placed or money is spent. For example, if the principal has a heart/passion for exceptional education then that department is given the world. If the principal is technology savvy then the school is inundated with the newest and greatest technology.

As I researched for this project, I found this to be an overwhelming area to dissect and tried to get to the bottom dollar and how funds are distributed. This process is tedious and would require many hours of research. There are just too many levels and contingencies.

Consequently, instead of parents fighting to get the same opportunities in their neighborhood schools they opt to ask for special assignments and sacrifice to provide transportation to selected schools because of what is perceived as a "better" school. This should not be the case. Education should be equal across the county. As a tax payer, parent and educator there should be a balance. It is blaringly not the case.

So the question would be, "What do we do about truly fully funding education?" We know that money is coming into the state, county, and finally the school. The effectiveness of the dollars is definitely in question.

We sadly hear the reply... *"What had happened was...,"* but do we really know the answer?

If You Learn, Teach
Reflections on Public School Funding
by Veronica Brown

A smiling, yet stern looking woman standing by a wooden door asked, "What's your name?" As a six year old girl being reared by her grandparents and mother's siblings, I respectfully replied, "Veronica Brown" as I stood impatiently wondering what unknown events this first day of school would bring. "Who's your daddy? Who's your mother? Where do you live?" I quickly responded to each question, somewhat embellishing each answer with details. I enjoyed relating how I was living on Gilliam's Farm while my mother earned money and went to school in New York. After a point, the woman with the twinkling eyes calmly stopped my colorful narrative by saying, "I taught your mother and your father. You will be a smart little girl." She then moved aside and ushered me with five other children into a large room. My attention was immediately drawn to the gigantic black big-bellied iron piece of furniture occupying the center of the room. I had never seen anything so huge, and I was immediately curious about its purpose. I remember two things about my first day of school: the iron piece of furniture and the teacher forecasting I would be smart. School seemed like it was going to be something good—maybe even fun.

It was this initial experience which motivated me to become an educator. A naïve part of me embraced the vision of every young child receiving an opportunity to learn. Through the years as I trudged from classroom to office to district headquarters, I came to realize individual student learning is not the primary business of public schools in this country.

Learning vs. Funding

Whether a school is labeled rural, urban or suburban, high-achieving or failing, there is never enough money to ensure every student receives a quality education. As a classroom teacher, I quickly learned to differentiate instruction by using my own money to purchase books and materials to meet the learning needs of my students. I learned how to write grants, enter contests, develop partnerships with colleagues, charm administrators and wrestle limited funds from PTA's. As I was initiated into the teaching profession, colleagues encouraged me to join a union, make no comments during faculty meetings, and never make critical comments about the school administration to parents. My world consisted of my classroom, my students and fellow teachers I encountered in the faculty lounge during my planning period. The issue of funding and the costs of educating a student were not something I was aware of, cared about, or thought impacted my teaching. My efforts were fruitful, because after a few years I was encouraged to move out of the classroom so I could have a broader impact on student learning. Suddenly my illusion was quickly dissipated. The expectation was I would become an instructional leader, who could teach and coach teachers in using the effective strategies I knew, which would promote student learning. Suddenly, my naiveté evolved into reality. I could not legally or morally tell colleagues to spend money on instructional tools and supplies; however, it was one of the most effective strategies I knew.

Public schools are primarily funded through property tax revenues and federal grants. The formula for how school districts receive and utilize funds has not changed too much since Horace Mann first introduced the idea of public education in Massachusetts. In 1838, in *The Common School Journal,* Mann introduced six main principles for public education: (1) the public should no longer remain ignorant; (2) education should be paid for, controlled and sustained by an interested public; (3) education will be best provided in schools that embrace children from a variety of backgrounds; (4) education must be non-sectarian; (5) education must be taught by the spirit, methods, and discipline of a free society; and (6) education should be provided by well-trained, professional teachers. Mann's ideas were quickly adopted by many states, and serves as the tenets for the approach to American education today. Early American educators have always argued the importance of education for teaching people how to think, to preserve democracy, and to ensure the productivity of the economy. Throughout American history there has been an emphasis on providing at least a rudimentary education for the poor.(21)

It was not until Brown v. Board of Education in 1954 that the funding of public schools became more of a legal than moral issue. The Supreme Court in ruling 'separate was not equal' in the educating of African American students in segregated schools, established a platform for a national debate on the equity of funding public schools. Expenditures on schooling are not equal from state to state. Within a state spending between districts also varies. Even today, the discourse continues as numerous school districts challenge state funding formulas through lawsuits. With the publishing of Jonathan Kozol's eye-opening book *Savage Inequalities* in 1991, the public outcry and government response to the inequity of public school funding created a plethora of financial adaptation and equalization efforts. In his book, Kozol describes a high school in Camden, New Jersey as having a computer room with 30 unusable computers, a broken boiler, a lab room with no equipment, and a 58 percent dropout rate. According to the Department of Education National Center for Educational Statistics for the years of Kozol's observations, New Jersey spent an average of $5,000 on educating each student. The Camden school Kozol visited received $4,000 per student. However, during the same time period nearby Cherry Hill spent over $6000 and Princeton spent over $8000 per student. "...some children are more equal than others in American public schools is an abomination, a national disgrace, and an ugly pustule on democracy's fair visage" laments Bob Chase, former president of the National Education Association.(22)

In reaction to myriad funding issues, and allegations of inequity, the second half of the twentieth century saw state and federal governments playing increasingly larger roles in the financial support of schooling. Despite the fact that in settling funding lawsuits state courts continued to emphasize student education as the duty of the state and its legislatures; it was clear new methods of funding were needed to ensure every student received an equal chance to obtain an adequate education.(23) Therefore, federal programs such as Title I, Head Start and after-school tutoring programs were developed to assist states in equalizing the allocation of funds. However, no significant financial reform for funding public schools was enacted.

Can we logically expect teachers to respond to the learning needs of each student, stay abreast of innovations in the field, continue to enroll in graduate courses, and participate in professional development activities to improve their knowledge base and teaching craft without examining the cost? As a high school principal who was committed to continual professional development opportunities for teachers, I found it extremely difficult to allocate funds for registration fees, substitutes, new technology equipment and the implementation of proven best instructional practices. The current Obama administration, as outlined in *A Blueprint for Reform: The Reauthorization of the Elementary and Secondary Education Act* describes 'greater equity' as: *every student a fair chance to succeed, and give principals and teachers the resources to support student success, we will call on school districts and states to take steps to ensure equity, by such means as moving toward comparability in resources between high and low-poverty schools.* It proposes to fund four reform models to ensure significant changes in the operation, governance, staffing, or instructional program of a school: transformation, turnaround, restart and school closure. School districts will be granted three year awards to fully and effectively implement one of the intervention models, and will be eligible for two additional years of funding to support ongoing school improvement. However, the administration's proposal does not attempt to redefine states' roles in equalizing funding between and within states. Rather, to ensure each student receives a well-rounded education, more resources will be provided to charter and private schools.(24)

Great Revenues Without Right...

Does the expenditure of more money equal better student achievement? Do states and school districts allocate funds wisely? The answers to these questions continue to serve as paradoxical explanations for how state legislatures, local school boards and school superintendents determine how to allocate increasingly limited funds dedicated to producing a high quality public education for every student. When one begins to examine all the stakeholders who demand to have a say in how money should be spent to educate students, it quickly becomes clear those who may know best how to make wise decisions and establish realistic priorities for funds are usually weak voices, or find themselves caught between self-preservation and dedication. Let me recount a specific situation to clarify the complexities of prioritizing and allocating educational resources.

In 2000, I served as principal of the largest high school in an urban city. Our student body consisted of 2600 students, grades 9-12, with a faculty and staff of 235. The administration consisted of seven assistant principals, an athletic director, a business manager and twenty department chairpersons. When assigned to the position, I was told I had three years to turnaround a failing school. Despite the urban blight surrounding the school, its population continued to grow. Why? The school district in an effort to increase student achievement, primarily the graduation rate, created application schools where students could focus on areas of interest like science, technology, the arts, and hospitality. These innovative schools received academic and financial support from local businesses, universities and private corporations. Students who were struggling academically, and/or did not pass entrance exams were relegated to attending a high school such as the one I was hired to lead.

Recognizing the daunting task facing me, the district and the state immediately provided me with a variety of resources: mentors, professional development opportunities for the faculty and staff, assistance with public relations, a ten member security staff, additional staff to work with special student populations and a team to monitor and facilitate school improvement efforts. I got busy.

By December of my first year, I had attended four funerals of students and staff members, created a school improvement team and wrestled a five year plan of action from the school improvement team, reorganized the administrative team, established procedures for collecting and analyzing student data, ordered and distributed operational and academic supplies, brought charges against two staff members for theft and fraud, patched numerous building maintenance problems, and spent the school's annual budget. As a result, I was summoned to the superintendent's office and told the school had overspent by more than $300,000. As principal, I was to determine how to eliminate the deficit, and continue to operate our school efficiently and effectively. My first thought was to release the business manager who was making about $90,000 a year; but I immediately recognized I was in an academic and financial quagmire.

So for the remainder of the year, I became a beggar who openly sought partnerships, participated in community organizations, visited churches, applied for grants, and increased building use to seven days a week and fifteen hours a day. With faculty and PTA approval, it was decided all new revenue would be spent on student learning needs only. The major costs of operating the school were not in my purview: teacher and staff salaries and benefits, replacement and repair costs, federally mandated class sizes for special student populations and an increasing student population. There were few complaints or concerns about a lack of funds from the staff or parents for they had no expectations for the elements needed to develop a high-achieving school. The faculty was accustomed to not having enough equipment, or supplies, and spent little time reflecting on what was needed to improve student achievement. The parents were more concerned about the safety of their children than the number of working computers in their classrooms. However, since I spent the majority of my professional career in suburban, wealthy school districts, I was frustrated by what I viewed as complacency and inequity.

As year two began, I was blessed with what I perceived as the ultimate opportunity. The school became eligible to apply for a Bill and Melinda Gates Foundation grant. In applying for the grant, the faculty and staff would have a chance to dream, plan, and act to improve the learning atmosphere, quality and success of our students. Even some naysayers, who had worked for more than 30 years in the district, began to embrace and anticipate change. After an intensive three months of planning, discussing, writing, revising, voting, scheduled and unscheduled site visits and panel interviews with parents, students, teachers and district administrators, and myself, the school was awarded a $10 million grant. It was the best news the city had received in years and I thought I could see a light at the end of the tunnel.

As with most grants, there were stipulations for compliance. The proposal budget and the final budget differed, but I felt no need to worry. Though the focus for the budget was shifted from student learning, the reasoning for doing so was logical and supported by the various constituents.

Sample school budget:

Proposal Budget	Estimated Cost
Instructional Initiatives	$ 2.5 million
Instructional supplies and equipment	$ 1.5 million
Professional Development	$ 500,000
Community and Student Initiatives	$ 500,000
Building Renovations	$ 1 million
Specialized Staffing	$ 4.0 million
Final Budget	Allocated Cost
Instructional Initiatives	$ 250,000
Instructional supplies and equipment	$ 400,000
Professional Development	$ 150,000
Community and Student Initiatives	$ 200,000
Building Renovations	$ 5.0 million
Specialized Staffing	$ 4.0 million

For example, in order to create more computer labs for the technology small learning community, the wiring, electrical and security systems in the school needed to be updated. The school's roof had been patched numerous times, but it was determined replacing the roof would be more energy efficient, and would eliminate repairs caused by periodic leaks. Built in the 1960's, the school was not in compliance with ADA regulations, so elevators and access ramps and entrances had to be installed. The school had 68 outside doors, all of which needed to have panic bars to comply with fire code regulations. Specialized staffing was needed to teach upper level academic classes to be offered in modern languages, science, and math. In addition, additional staff was hired to implement individual education plans for students with special learning needs, and staff to teach and monitor special programs such as ROTC and a community daycare center required additional funding. The spirit of the grant was to augment school district resources, not supplant them.

By the end of my second year as principal, I was deeply enmeshed in a political struggle between the superintendent, members of the school board and some members of the community. Questions about the allocation of resources began to surface. Specifically, some prominent members of the community thought it was foolish to sink scarce resources into a failing school with no proven record of achievement. In my first year as principal, the ninth grade class consisted of 1500 ninth graders, the senior class 138 with 110 graduating, and a passing rate of under 50% on state achievement tests. Though the attendance rate increased from 40% to 70% in two years, it was still well below the district and state average. Why should a failing school be given more autonomy to expend funds, make curricular changes and shift faculty without proven results?

Change is a slow process and documenting academic progress is even slower. However, the superintendent was pressured more intensely to show improvement results, thus my position shifted from instructional leader to political scapegoat. As the appearance of our school improvement data became more stagnant under closer scrutiny, decisions about how to spend the grant funds were shifted to district administrators. The responsibility for coordinating projects was shifted from the school to the district level. Thus began the unraveling of a year of incremental progress. The school's wiring was upgraded, however a month later during a violent thunderstorm, one fourth of the building roof collapsed, destroying the new alarm system. This obvious lack of coordination was met with much finger pointing, but no solutions and no positive results. When the school board voted to fire the superintendent, it became evident there would be a change in philosophy, but most significantly, a return to what we were, rather than what we were becoming.

Faced with rising educational costs, and legally strapped to district revenue limits set by state aid and property tax formulas, the district's school board responded like so many of its counterparts by enacting measures to cut costs through eliminating and lessening academic programs, delaying and foregoing the purchase of technology, equipment, textbooks and supplies, and postponing school maintenance and renovation projects. In an effort to create equity, what was once considered school-based decisions became district ones. Even though the scenario previously described dealt with grant funds, public perception and school board actions emphasized the current revenue allocation quandary that can only be resolved through a reassessing and reforming of the public school funding structure.

"A Paddle Here, A Paddle There,
The Canoe Stays Still."
Sierra Leone Proverb

In this brief discussion, I have outlined some of the financial issues facing public education today. There is not enough money to ethically, legally or morally meet the varied learning needs of students legally compelled to receive some type of schooling. So what remedies can be used to adapt to the continuing financial crisis facing public education? As previously mentioned, the Obama administration is not proposing specific changes in the traditional formulas states and districts use to fund public education. Instead, *A Blueprint for Reform* proposes to positively impact student learning by directing and monitoring the way states and districts prioritize funding for education. "We must support families, communities, and schools working in partnership to deliver services and supports that address the full range of student needs." The concept of partnerships is not new, however, directing federal funds to support and sustain effective collaborations is a different approach. The administration proposes to provide competitive 'funding streams' to enable state and local districts to be innovative and flexible in rewarding school improvement and the monitoring of revenue expenditures. The use of funding streams will allow the blending of funds from different categories and require less red tape to secure them. Specifically, proposal objectives cite the following new approaches:

- Providing incentives for a Race to the Top among states and districts willing to take on ambitious, comprehensive reforms.

- Developing, validating, and scaling up promising and proven educational strategies to improve student outcomes.

- Expanding educational options to increase choice within the public school system through high-performing new schools and meaningful public school choice. (24)

What far-reaching changes for local schools will these approaches create if implemented? First, recognizing the successful implementation of any change will begin with school personnel, teachers and administrators. The issues surrounding the policies and practices governing teacher unions, salaries and benefits, evaluation and promotion quickly rise to the surface. Teacher unions compete with other public service unions such as those representing fire and police departments for limited public funds. Yet, the public demands a different type of accountability for school personnel. Whereas the positive use of public funds is reaffirmed when police departments report a decrease in crime, and the media streams a wealth of visual images denoting heroic fire and rescue workers in dangerous situations, school personnel continue to report dismal graduation rates and lowering standardized test scores. Public perception is clearly created by issues of accountability and proven public service. Therefore, school personnel need to rethink and reframe guidelines for the hiring, promoting and evaluating of teachers and administrators. More accountability is needed.

Traditional in house practices need to change. During my tenure as a teacher, it was not unusual to hear those teachers labeled to be the best proudly recount their high failure rates. In fact, the so-called 'hard' teacher was the one who failed students. The traditional practice of assigning new teachers to the most difficult classes is another practice that defeats change. In many schools, the more veteran teachers receive the better classes not necessarily because of their skills, but due to their longevity. Too often in many school districts, administrators are selected and promoted because of their political connections and reputations for maintaining student discipline. A part of determining if limited funds are spent wisely is ensuring the right people with the needed skills are appropriately matched to key positions. Critics of merit pay, bonus incentives and other strategies for rewarding teacher and administrator accountability have buried their heads in the sand.

Second, there needs to be more educational options and programs for parents, universities and the broader community to partner with. Charter schools, community institutions and other educational initiatives can address the varied needs of our students. It is not realistic to assume today's large public schools can be expected to provide the best education for every type of student entitled to enter their doors. The state of Florida has initiated several innovative instructional programs, but its FCAT scores and graduation rates are low, especially in urban school districts.

For example, in Orlando there is a large high school located across the street from Universal Studios. The school offers TV/Video production classes, but at this point, receives limited resources from the private enterprise. Another program allows high school seniors to be dually enrolled in the community college during their senior year. With successful completion of two years at the community college, students are guaranteed entrance into a local four year college. This road mapping of students' career paths is proving to be a successful strategy for increasing student successful college graduation. Partnerships need to span the length of a student's educational journey. A very successful charter school in New York City guides students from preschool to college. A parochial high school in urban California reports a 100% graduation rate for the past four years, with all students being accepted into college. There are numerous success stories, however, the strategies and techniques used to create such scholastic accomplishments are still perceived as exceptions, rather than the norm. Widespread educational options for families and students can ensure limited funds are spent more effectively and efficiently.

Finally, more resource building and use of funds to develop long range and sustainable instructional practices is needed. In the scenario described earlier, the grant was to be expended in three years. Often it takes two to three years to plan and begin to implement needed change. Yet, before the implementation stage is fully enacted the program and/or initiative is due for a results evaluation. The rapid change in district superintendents, the election of school boards and the constant moving and removal of local school administrators, especially in urban districts, are all barriers to ensuring resources are spent prudently and wisely. Change is a systematic and often slow process. In public schools the processes for change and funding need to be blended, and monitored simultaneously. This will require a totally new method for how funds are prioritized, allocated and ultimately spent.

Extracurricular Activities

"From the Sidelines"

A conversation with
Coach "Law" Johnson, Jr. and Ushanda Pauling

Lawrence has been a high school and semi-pro football coach for about 10 years. He has coached in both urban and suburban settings.

Coach, please share an occasion when you were "schooled" by a student.

"Jeff," summer 2007, in the middle of practices twice a day; my backup quarterback was messing up every play. For a straight hour, the messing up continued and his only reply every time addressed was "Yes sir." Once practiced ended, I called him to the front of the huddle. I told the team this is the type of player that I want; after all that yelling he only ever said, "Yes sir." The team was shocked.

No matter how bad things got, Jeff was always in control of his emotions. That took a lot to rise above what he felt and the embarrassment in front of other teammates. The lesson for me was self-control. He maintained composure during all that. That was a huge lesson for the entire coaching staff; everybody had gotten on to him that day. After that he gained the respect of the team and the entire coaching staff and before the season's end, he became the starting quarterback.

What is the single best change that could be made to improve the current educational system?

I don't know if there is a single change but one that I can think of would be, for any student in the school with a Grade Point Average (GPA) below a 2.0, suspended more than five days, and having more than 10 absences in one class, would be placed on the following academic improvement plan:

- One semester (2 nine weeks) to bring it up to 1.0 (if below a 1.0) and
- One additional semester to bring it to a 2.0.

If they were successful, they could remain at the school. If they were not successful then they would be dismissed from the school and another school would be developed to serve those students. The research that I have done and my experience being a School Resource Officer (SRO) shows that kids in this category are typically disciplinary problems. The disciplinary issue that they cause interrupts other student's rights to education and the disrupter should not override the other person's right to learn. In my view, they have forfeited their rights. I would want to preserve and protect the rights of those that are putting forth the effort to apply themselves behaviorally and academically and not to leave the others behind but to recognize that they may be better suited for a different structure; maybe vocational training.

Is there ever a conflict of interest between teaching and coaching?

There isn't a conflict on the surface. I say that because you see situations where you have a star player that is coming up short academically, which would affect his eligibility and you may fudge some numbers so that he passes and remains eligible. If the overall interest is for him or her as a person you should let them sit out because they need to feel the sting of being ineligible and whatever is not happening in the classroom needs to be addressed. If there is a learning disability, then the coach should help to overcome that and whatever the student-athlete may need.

What are some critical reasons to promote sports within the current educational system?

Let me give you one good reason, for football anyway. In my experience in the state of Florida and in South Georgia, football is a good identifier for what kind of school climate you have. A lot of schools get credit for being good schools based on what the team looks like. It is usually true because the pride around the school is usually based upon how the football team performs. There is a different atmosphere and a different pride when the football team is a winning team instead of a losing one.

It also gives students a way to release a lot of that pent up energy from being required to be still and quiet in a classroom. A good coach can properly channel that in all aspects of a student's life to promote success on the field. A student's ability to manage those things impacts their abilities on the field. For example, at one school I had a bi-weekly progress report that the position coaches handed out. They called the parents of the players and let them know what was on the report and that it needed to be looked at and signed signifying that they had been notified of the students' academic standing. Players were deemed temporarily ineligible until it was returned and signed. We conducted one every two weeks whereas the school only required it every three weeks. This kept us ahead of the school and gave us an opportunity to build relationships with the parents and it built a partnership with the three links (class, home, and sport).

Athletics is an avenue to higher education. If you are in the 0.1%, athletics can be an avenue to professional career.

How does a coach keep perspective/ balance of a person being a student- athlete?

Keeping perspective requires having the mindset that although the objective is to win whatever sport; coaching for me is "man building". What I mean by that is my objectives are bigger and longer than the season. I am looking at that young man three years after he's left me or high school. Winning and losing translates into keeping a job but to me the more you put in to a player helps me keep my perspective. If they are having issues with team rules or school rules, I can't waiver on the discipline because I look at NFL stars and the problems they have. I believe that they probably had those same problems on their high school teams and the coaches were more focused on winning than on "man building".

I want my players to go off to college and have their coaches call me and express their happiness to have them.

Why do you feel all extracurricular activities are not promoted equally? For example, arts programs versus athletics.

Money, plain and simple. Sports generating money get the most publicity. Another part is about the interest in certain things like the band and chorus. If you're at a school that doesn't traditionally have a good band, children are less apt to want to participate. Even if some participate there won't be that many.

Having a coach who has a winning track record, makes a big difference. At one school we had 180 students.

Kids attention is devoted in so many different places now that some extra-curricular activities in school aren't even attractive.

And the staff that it takes to run these things are usually not compensated or are not compensated decently. This translates into people not wanting to do the activity. Or, if they do the activity, they don't put their heart into it, then the activity gets dropped.

Does being a student - athlete have privileges others students do not have?

Yes, they do! For a college student-athlete, particularly football, there are millions of dollars made off the backs of these athletes. So, depending on the sport, they have to juggle school work, travel, and playing the sport. Most non-athletic students aren't juggling all of these different things at once. There are occasions where people wouldn't know about the school if it weren't for the student-athletes. Not that they deserve special treatment, but it happens because of the sacrifices they make. Just the fact that they may have to travel in the middle of the week or a couple of times a week to represent the school and in between doing all of that complete school work and study for tests; that's a huge sacrifice. That's why the school gives you money to do it.

Legal or illegal privileges? They usually get first dibs on getting class schedules set to accommodate practice time. Someone on the coaching staff usually has some clout with schedule makers. Depending on the school's resources, they have tutors assigned to the athletes that usually do all of their work for them. Non-athletes don't have that. Athletes are often outfitted with apparel because of the schools affiliation with a brand. Illegal activity, can't speak on that. I don't want to say. It happens; times when other people are doing your work, taking your test, etcetera.

High school also has privileges depending on the sports again, those students are kind of the ambassadors of the school. Depending on how influential the student-athletes' are can determine the makeup of the school. There are not too many privileges to give a high schooler. They don't travel midweek so the same work and testing practices don't happen. Depending on the seriousness of the coach, they are given more time to do work. Academic problems are caught a lot faster due to eligibility requirements. Sometimes you have situations where coaches can keep kids out of trouble and influence things to keep a kid from getting suspended. I have seen where students didn't want to go to a particular class so they spend that class period with the coach or come back from lunch and to prevent another tardy, get the coach to write a pass to get into class.

Some of the extreme cases from the past with star quarterbacks are not happening as much in 2010. There were times where a blind eye was turned, but not as much now.

What are some challenges for coaching in the current school environment?

1. School administration not committed to successful athletics. This is done not by giving the coach the proper tools to do the job; equipment, uniforms, locker rooms, etc. In my coaching experience, I have had to fight all of administration, including the athletic department for a field house (a locker room facility for the players and storage for equipment). When administration is not committed to successful programs those things aren't priority.

2. Having a guidance counselor dedicated to student athletes to ensure that they are on track with credits and graduate. I made my guidance counselors work. I required my athletes to meet with counselors to make sure they were taking the right courses to be on track for their college study goals, given information about dual enrollment programs, registered for the clearinghouse, and making sure that standardized testing requirements have been met for eligibility. Things that athletes need tend to get pushed to the back burner when people aren't dedicated to help athletes with their specific needs.

3. Not having proper facilities or them not being modernized or adequate to the standard to the amount of student athletes you might have.

4. Allocation of financial resources. Principals don't have a standard method, they allocate them as they see fit, not based on what's actually necessary.

5. Income opportunity for the sport is high in some places but in other places not so much. It's easier to attract quality coaches when there is more opportunity to make money.

6. Not being able to have quality assistant coaches. A lot of time people are coaching on teams because they are a teacher at the school, and that doesn't make them a good coach. I don't understand why these two things are put together. In some places, it's a requirement to be a teacher if you want to coach and that doesn't make sense to me. They are two different types of teaching. In a lot of cases a coach can reach student athletes in ways far greater than a classroom teacher.

Notes from the Hardwood: Education and Athletics

by Ushanda Pauling

Describe a time when you saw or heard of another educator being "schooled" by a student.

This story is not about educators but a group of adults that were "schooled" by a team of students. I remember when I coached a competitive girls' basketball team; the parents of my team were actually "schooled" by the team as a whole. My coaching philosophy has always been to develop the character of players along with build on their athletic skills. I was coaching a pre-teen team at the time. Anyone who knows anything about adolescence has an understanding that cultivating female athletes at this stage of development involves far more than focusing on running plays and showing up for games. I was teaching, constantly. Most of the parents initially brought their daughters to me because they showed some aptitude in the sport. What they had not considered were those little intricacies of building an athlete, competitor, young lady, teammate, friend, multi-tasker, discipline, structure, and so much more.

We traveled out of town from time to time and I made it a practice to do certain things with the girls to facilitate transference of these life lessons. I would mix them up at meals and require them to sit with different teammates. When we had extra time at the hotel I called team huddles that had nothing to do with ball but everything to do with building up the team, their individual confidence, and their receiving support about life issues.

Fast forward several months to a parent meeting where it was announced to me that I would no longer be coaching the team. A few parents, who were trying to make their daughters become the next Candace Parker or Diana Taurasi, decided I wasn't pushing the girls hard enough and pounding drills and plays into them. I was floored and deeply saddened all at the same time. I was ambushed by the few, while the others sat timidly.

When that coaching experience was done I went on to coach other teams and was a conditioning coach for some of those same players individually.

Out of that entire bunch I remained closest with three of the youngest girls on the team. One of them is well on her way to becoming an inventor, is an incredible athlete, and will graduate college with honors. The other two went on to become top performers in the area, gleaning tremendous media attention and multiple scholarship offers. They will have graduated with honors. Those three youth stuck to me like glue after my coaching position was removed. Their parents called me to work with them in the summers and off seasons to condition them and develop their skills. But most importantly the girls called me. They called me for help with their technical skills, they wanted me at their games, they asked my advice for things with their parents, coaches, teachers, and peers; all of those life lessons that I had been instilling off the court. Their parents even called for me to come and talk to them at different times on their adolescent journey and sent invitations for birthday parties and graduations. In the end, the girls "schooled" them all. Their voices spoke volumes but no one had ever asked them. Some dropped completely from the sport and decided to do other things. When they got the opportunity to speak they gravitated towards what was most helpful to them; not who put WINS and LOSSES on the scoreboard.

Is there ever a conflict of interest between teaching and coaching?

In terms of what should actually occur, the roles are closely related; however, in reality, they can at times, be worlds apart and in direct conflict.

In some schools I have witnessed classroom teachers, Physical Education (PE) coaches and sports coaches at odds. Classroom teachers shouting on one end that students are being distracted from learning and coaches on the other end shouting that team play and participation is assisting them in learning.

I can remember in high school, my coach would write passes for us to leave class and do special projects to prepare for a game or tournament. At one point, one of my teachers got very upset and felt that I was not taking her class serious enough. I must admit, I did not like that particular teacher but I took my grades very serious. She thought I was completely blowing off her class but I actually was getting more assistance from another teammate and even sometimes my coach by not being in her classroom. I was more distracted by my dislike for her than letting someone else tutor me outside of the classroom. Fortunately for me, my coach was a bit of a bulldog and continued to write passes for me. She had never abused the passes but she was aware that if she was going to take me out of a class, that may be one to consider doing so.

What are 5 reasons to promote sports within the current educational system?

1. Again we have tons research that is not being used to the fullest. There are various articles and studies that have revealed the importance of physical activity and its impacts on learning; yet we continue to make cuts in physical education and sports programs across the country. You have to start asking, why? Do we really care what the research says or are we researching just for the sake of researching?

2. Childhood Obesity - the documentary film world has enlightened us all to the causes and factors contributing so heavily to our food and nutrition intake. We have the fitness world telling us and selling to us constantly products, ideas and services that would help us address our health and where it has lead; a generation that is projected to die before their parents! Are we outraged yet? Clearly we can't be, because we haven't addressed it immediately. The health of children in this country is as serious as a natural disaster; it is its own natural disaster.

3. Building life skills; encouraging the practice of thinking, planning, multi-tasking, teamwork, social skills, and discipline.

4. In 1996, Ashley Koehn referenced the NIKE: IF YOU LET ME PLAY Campaign:

    > If you let me play sports
    > I will like myself more,

> I will have more self-confidence,
> I will be 60 percent less likely to get breast cancer;
> I will suffer less depression.
> I will be more likely to leave a man who beats me.
> I will be less likely to get pregnant
> I will learn what it means to be strong.
> If you let me play sports. (25)

5. Promoting sports can lead to increased parent involvement which would ultimately strengthen families.

How does a coach keep perspective/ balance of a person being a student- athlete?

It is no mistake the term is student-athlete; this automatically guides coaches to where the focus should be. I believe that coaches at all education levels should have athletic programs designed with the student's academic success being the primary focus.

As a former basketball player and Amateur Athletic Union (AAU) coach, the athletics piece is very important but I also know that making sure that players succeed academically has to be paramount. Statistically, we know that only a small percentage of student-athletes are able to move on to professional level sports. As coaches, our perspective has to be grounded in reality. Pushing athletes to peek performance and striving for winning team records is wonderful, however, the true reality of school sports is that the majority of our student-athletes will not advance on to the professional level and must therefore have training or an academic background to help transition them to work and adulthood.

Why do you feel all extracurricular activities are not promoted equally? For example arts programs versus athletics.

What happens in the world of young people is, for the most part, a direct symptom, outcome, or reflection of what is happening in our society at large. Promotion follows money. There is big money spent and made in the sports arena. Depending on the geographic area, the focus on a particular sport maybe stronger in one place versus another. We see this at the national level among professional sports.

Many have said it time and time again, what we value is reflected by how we spend our money. Money also manipulates us to change our minds or becomes the basis of our decisions.

I believe there are many young people talented and gifted in areas that are not sports related. However, when you attend the school open house, unless you attend an advanced arts program or magnet school with a concentration in arts, you are sure to miss the appeal of such extracurricular activities. But you cannot blame young people for their oversight in these seemingly free choice activities. This practice is showcased in our culture at almost every turn. When you look at product marketing and advertisement, frequently the spokesperson is an athlete. There are actresses/actors that promote products but our sports figures are who we rally around. If I am the kid with little to no athletic prowess, the options for me seem pretty narrow, but I can join the masses and be a paying spectator.

As with most things, if you transfer the money, the people will follow.

Does being a student-athlete have privileges others student(s) do not have? If yes, please describe.

Remember my experience in high school with the classroom teacher that I didn't care for? That is definitely an example of a privilege not afforded to the entire student body. Not every student had access to a 'get out of class pass when they came across a teacher they didn't like.

* Travel and exposure to other people and environments. Through my sports participation I was able to see other cities and states and get a little taste of how others live. That exposure gave me a greater understanding of myself, but also prevented me from being narrow-minded about people and the world.

* Life skills development can be acquired a number of ways but the sports arena was an ongoing practice ground for me. Day in and day out I was taught cooperative play, being part of something larger than myself, contributing to the success of a group, listening, practicing tolerance and acceptance, and an overall understanding that there

really is not equality among people. I learned other practical skills like money management (after a few trips when I spent money way too fast), doing laundry, living with others (even just a couple of days with another athlete can seem like years), sharing, responsibility, discipline, commitment, study skills (there were a lot of classes that I had to rely on my notes to help because I missed class or couldn't meet with a study group).

What are some challenges for coaching in the current school environment?

1. Inexperienced coaches.

   The sport is being offered, someone needs to coach it. The stipend is so insignificant that an experienced coach may pass on the offer, leaving the potential coaching pool very limited.

2. Inexperienced student-athletes.

   On a school team you pretty much have to work with what you have at the school. Coaches and team members try and recruit student-athletes but there are limits to the success of that. I served for many years as a coach with recreational leagues, which for the most part, were developmental and taught only the basics of a sport. The way that things are set up now, a kid that participates in a league like that moves on to a middle/ junior high school team (which in many cases has 20 kids on the team and the season is less than 15 games), and then to high school. When we look at most developmental leagues they operate on an 'everyone can play for the exposure' philosophy and some skill development occurs. But the reality is, the time to develop skill and abilities cannot truly be fostered in this type of league. That means that young people wanting more have to seek out another source. All of these things are fine but then we are back to an access and equality issue. Those issues are compounded when we get to the middle/ junior high school level because the budget cuts have significantly impacted the sports seasons. 10- 12 games is hardly an appropriate amount of time to make any real change; especially at such a developmentally radical time period. The really talented kids sail through all of this as well as those who are able to access additional opportunities. The not so talented or ones that have never played at all really struggle. The kids who are not able to play on organized teams sometimes have an extremely difficult time because they have never been coached and don't have competitive experience.

3. Non-cohesive teaching and coaching staffs.

   The great divide over which is more important. Each is working so hard to prove that their role is more important instead of looking for more commonalities and ways to join forces.

4. Limited financial resources within schools altogether.

   Travel budgets, uniform costs, equipment shortages, and school districts that cut in all the wrong places.

5. Outside sports leagues, such as AAU and other recreation leagues, have gained notoriety and are able to pull in a diverse group of athletes, making them incredibly competitive and having much more opportunity to travel and compete due to individual funding and sponsorships. This becomes especially important when you are skilled and want to develop your talents to its highest potential while gaining exposure for potential college scholarship opportunities. If you live in a city or state that is not known for producing high performing athletes, playing for your local school team doesn't generally get you noticed, by college recruiters.

6. Time.

   Practice time and the length of the season. Again this goes back to finances. I can remember when I was in high school; the boys and girls basketball teams had to switch practice times each month in order to use the only gym that we had. So some weeks we practiced immediately after school, while other weeks we had to wait for the boys team to finish.

7. Recruitment of knowledgeable coaches.

   Many great coaches do not actually reside within the school walls. There is not an active recruiting process, it is a haphazard effort that essentially waits for someone to take an interest in or administration appoints someone to oversee the youth for them to at least have the opportunity to play. I have seen several examples where the school doesn't have a qualified person to coach so they put an all call out for someone who is at least willing to coach the group. I have also seen the example of the good hearted coach that may not be knowledgeable about a particular sport but has a willing heart; so they become the coach of multiple sports and you see them on every team's sideline.

Bottom of the Bucket: Education and Economics

by Lynnette Stallworth

Because matters of finance are key to the issue of education, it is important to offer a bird's-eye view of economics. This overview is intended to help all who are participating in education transformation to have a similar language related to what is happening in order to talk about global, national and local economics.

Economics and education are linked as are siblings in a family. By definition, economics is the management of resources. The goal of education is to gain knowledge in a broad scope of living essentials.

It is now imperative for education stakeholders to gain what is called the "new literacy". This "new literacy" is being aware enough to be comfortable navigating the layers that is the global economy. Up to this point in time now the public discourse has been stuck on teacher's compensation as it relates to local budgets. The "new literacy" goes beyond local municipalities and conflict with unions and state. These have been arguably more political than purely economic.

Keep in mind, the goals within education include readying students for gainful employment. Without an increased understanding of economics, education is at a loss, being out-of-step with what, where and how prospective employment is to be found. Should there be any doubt, consider this "Great Recession" where jobs have moved to other countries and jobs that have vanished due to technology. Education must become futuristically laser focused on what is emerging on the job/career front. There needs to be an "end-goal" in order to successfully design a road-map. In education, where are the efforts to produce gainfully employed individuals?

Global Matters

Almost nothing is simple; especially as it relates to finances, let alone worldwide finances. Here is a "birds-eye" view of the major participants in what are global economic financial alliances.

Bilderberg Group

Unofficially based at the University of Leiden in the Netherlands, this is an extremely elite group that outsiders know close to nothing about its form or function. What is believed to be known is it came into being around 1954. It is by invitation only that approximately 140 political, economic and financial world renowned individuals gather once every twelve months. Their agenda is not shared with the public nor is there any statement of actions taken or considered. Bilderberg Group is selected – not elected.

Group of 7 (G-7) and Group of 8 (G-8)

Do these groups sound familiar or ring-a-bell? Perhaps you've heard of their planned meeting including location, agenda and decisions in the news.

They meet a number of times each year to review and create economic policies. This in part means the group determines the management of finances in a systematic way. The groups are made up of finance ministers/secretaries for specific industrialized countries.

Originally, there was the G-6 (1975). Then came the G-7 (1976) and in 1997 the G-8. Currently the G-7 is made up of: Canada, France, Germany, Italy, Japan, United Kingdom and the United States of America. By adding Russia to the list, it became the G-8. However the G-8 unlike the G-7 has heads of nations as participants.

Group of 20 (G-20)

This group is made up of two major economies. The configuration is different than G-7 and G-8 due to the G-20 seating of the European Union (EU), which is a group within the group. There are 19 countries plus the EU.

This group's purpose is said to be consultants on international financial systems. What is most interesting about the G-20 is some of its profile. Together, the G-20 represents:
- 85% of the World's Gross National Product (GNP)

- 80% of the World's Trade
- 2/3rd of the World's Population

The membership includes, Argentina, Australia, Brazil, Canada, China, the European Union, France, Germany, India, Indonesia, Italy, Japan, Russia, Saudi Arabia, South Africa, South Korea, Turkey, United Kingdom and the United States of America.

Group of 24 (G-24)

This group established in 1971, comprised of three world regions – Africa, Latin America and the Caribbean; and Asia members are two-tiered. These are ministers of finance and central bank governors; and others designated as deputies. This group meets two times a year.

The member countries (and EU) send finance ministers/secretaries and representatives from their central bank governors. There is a rotation of which country hosts the G-20 meetings.

The World Economic Forum (WEF)

It was founded to bring world businesses together for the purpose of problem-solving as it impacts stakeholders. The WEF is about 40 years old. Based in Geneva, Switzerland, it is considered a non-profit organization. Its annual meeting is known as the Davos Conferences and convenes in Davos, Switzerland. Their gatherings are public, well attended and covered by media each year.

International Monetary Fund (IMF)

It says of itself, there are three main functions of the IMF. It functions as a monitor of economic and financial crisis prevention. The IMF is a lender to countries in serious debt situations. And thirdly, the IMF offers technical assistance in areas of research and statistics. One can say, in that respect, the IMF is a specialized world educator.

This organization is made up of some 187 countries and was founded circa 1945. The IMF has an executive board, which is comprised of representatives from the member countries. The G-7, G-20 and G-24 serves in advisory capacity.

The IMF is said to be fully accountable and transparent. What is not clear is the seeming redundancy of the IMF and the World Bank.

The World Bank

In the economic community, The World Bank and the International Monetary Fund are sometimes spoken of simultaneously and/or interchangeably. They are seen as "twins" because of their story similarity.

They were established at the very same time and have virtually the same structures. They have the same membership.

The two immediate differences are: the World Bank's singular goal is to reduce poverty by lending to developing countries for capital projects, the other difference is their address, although both are home-based in Washington, D.C.

Remember almost nothing is simple and so it is with The World Bank and the International Monetary Fund being almost identical.

North America Free Trade Agreement (NAFTA)

NAFTA is spoken of often. It is in a category all its own. NAFTA is a uniquely regional economic/financial relationship among Canada, The United States of America and Mexico. NAFTA is not global and it is not exclusively that of America.

It originally was Canada and the USA in 1994. In 1999 it became Canada, USA and Mexico. The purpose of NAFTA is explained as gaining greater purchasing power by being a trading block and resolving economic/financial conflict between and amongst one another. One might be helped to view the purpose of NAFTA as similar to Organization of Petroleum Exporting Countries (OPEC). There is much debate and controversy surrounding NAFTA.(26)

Economics: Part 2

These entities you may think are the proverbial "They" so often referred to when frustration of disenfranchisement stares one directly in the face. One would be only partially correct in believing the participants in all the "alphabet soup" above are all the "Theys".

There are others who attach themselves to form a more perfect and powerful "They". They include the heads and former heads of the member nations, as well as heads of the mega corporations, companies, businesses, all around the globe. No longer imagining – these are "They".

United States of America

The Federal Reserve (The Fed)

This is the central banking system for the whole country. It is the bank-of-banks. The Fed was established circa 1913. It, among many things, sets the interest rate from which other financial institutions take the queue to set their interest rates.

The president appoints the Board of Governors which numbers seven, with The Fed Chairman being highly influential in directing the entire economy of the USA.

The United States Treasury

The United States Treasury was established by Alexander Hamilton in 1789 to keep track of all monies. Most commonly, "The Treasury" is known for literally making the money to be in circulation. This agency within The Treasury is called The Mint. Some other agencies include the Internal Revenue Services (IRS), administration grants and loans, savings products (U.S. Saving Bonds) and auction division. This division auctions off items taken from legal proceeds. There are about 300 auctions held every year. Also under The Treasury is the Troubled Asset Relief Program (TARP).

The Treasury functions from the mandate of, 'Maintain a strong economy and create economic and work opportunities, combat threats and protect the integrity of the financial system...manage the U.S. Government's finance and resources effectively.'

The Federal Deposit Insurance Corporation (FDIC)

This organization was created in 1933 to respond to bank failures of the 1920's and 1930's. As its name says, this organization is the insurance company of the United States banking system. While banks continue to fail, the individual accounts (with specific rules) are by-in-large safe-guarded. Not all financial instruments are insured by the FDIC.

The following Federal Government Mortgages make loans for buying houses:

- Federal Housing Authority (FHA)
- U.S. Department of Housing and Urban Development (HUD)
- Federal National Mortgage Association (Fannie Mae)
- Federal Home Loan Mortgage Corporation (Freddie Mac)

They have specific requirements regarding whom a loan may be made to and what type of home they are allowed to finance. Not everyone qualifies for these mortgage loans, and not every property qualifies for being financed by these lenders.

Wall Street

"Wall Street" is a collect-all name for investments in America. The business of stocks, bonds, annuities and other financial instruments are bought and traded through various exchanges. There are many exchanges.

The oldest in the U.S. is the Philadelphia Exchange. The two largest American exchanges are the National Association of Securities Dealers Automated Quotations (NASDAQ) and the New York Stock Exchange (NYSE). The two largest exchanges, NASDAQ and NYSE plus the Dow Jones Industrial Average (DJIA) are seen commonly in daily public reporting.

Looking behind the curtains there are pending economic happenings that will vastly impact the current economic and financial system.

Those involved in decision-making on the global economy level speak in terms of "...value added countries....knowledge-based countries." It is at this junction America is in a very tenuous position. Given the state of the current economy including the unimaginable federal debt and global low-ranking education of America, what then, is America's "value added" and "knowledge base" in global terms?

It is projected the Group of 7 (G-7) will soon be overshadowed by the world's largest emergency economics, such as China. *G-7 will fade as the likely Emerging 7 (E-7) rises to leadership.*

Other significant changes on the horizon include the creation of a global currency. "Currency merge" has been a topic amongst members of the Group of 20 (G-20) and the World Economic Forum (WEF) over the past two years. *Unified currencies* are being urged to begin with the United States and Europe. That would mean a brand new currency of the dollar and the euro.

This new global currency is to replace the dollar as the worlds' foreign exchange reserve currency of choice.

In light of the dollar's fall in 2007/2008 and the "Great Recessions" global impact, a *Global Redesign Initiative* has been put in places, since 2010. As most believe the alliances cannot return to business as usual.

Then there is the North American Free Trade Agreement (NAFTA). In its short-lived life, NAFTA has become a major spin-off called the <u>NAFTA</u> Superhighway. The NAFTA Superhighway is said to be responsible for creating the North American Union. The physical roadways link Canada, the United States and Mexico. These roadways may be proposed as toll roads in the near future.

Geographic Details of the NAFTA Super Highway

Interstate-35
*   Mexican Border in Laredo, Texas to Duluth, Minnesota; then connect Minnesota Highways into Canada

Interstate-20
*   Kansas City, Missouri off I-35 to Pembina, North Dakota; then into Manitoba Highway (Canada)

Interstate-94
*   Picks up on shared U.S. side of Blue Water Bridge in Port Huron, Michigan; Crosses I-69 (Marshall, MI); I-65 (Gary, IN); I-80 (S.

Holland, IN); I-55 (Chicago, IL); I-43 (Milwaukee, WI); I-39 (Madison, WI); I-35 (St. Paul, Min); I-29 (Fargo, ND) and I-90 (Billings, Mt).

Railway infrastructure also includes pipelines and fiber optics.(26)

The Wall Street alert is: *"nothing has changed"* or is planned to change despite the economic and financial crises termed, " The Great Recession".

Financially Failed Communities

As concern ensues for commonwealths, states, countries and other municipalities throughout these United States, there is a trend of strained, deficient, even bankrupt budgets. No need to explain how this economic and financial issue affects education. What is critical is who and how education is paying the price for lack of funding. A very real cycle is in motion. High unemployment has led to low property tax receipts. In the haste to make budget adjustments, dismissal of teachers is on the rise, which will mean more low tax receipts. In the survival of this economic and financial storm, school children are hung-out to dry.

The relationship between employment and tax revenue (personal & property) is moving quickly downward. Schools at one time were ranked by being in high property tax areas. This is the "location, location, location" value theory. With real estate in such poor condition, the funding for education is worse than ever.

Personal Economics and Finances

All the above brings to center stage where the "rubber meets the road" for you, your family, your life. This is where your personal economics and finances come into play. We all fall into an economic status. Some are at the tippy-top, being wealthy and others are upper class, upper-middle class, middle class, or lower-income. The poverty level is off the radar completely as homeless and jobless.

Only you can know how you and your household arrived in your given category. Only you can project whether your status is secure or insecure: moving upward, staying as is, or possibly facing a downward turn in the future.

Whatever your economic and financial situation, we all participate in the comprehensive picture presented here. No one escapes. As the wizard, at some point in time there has been or is a savings, checking, money market, mortgage, credit card, certificate of deposit, insurance policy, 401K, IRA, stock, bond or annuity in your name. This means we are all participants in concerns over interest rates. Remember interest rates, values and earnings are set by the much larger, behind the curtain, decisions of the current economic system.

So how does this speak to education and education transformation? To this point in time, education has been seen as a "taker" versus "contributor". The bottom-line economically and financially would, "They" term education as a liability versus an asset.

> "The way you see people is the way you treat them,
> and the way you treat them is what they become."
> Joahnn Von Goethe

The challenge, in purely economic and financial terms, is shifting education

from the D-list to the A-list. Education can then be seen as crucial to the infrastructure of the United States funding for consistent, uncompromised quality standards.

"The sea has drowned the fish," is an African saying to signify everything has gone wrong; extreme upheaval. The horrible downturn in the economy is different than past episodes. This is a 21st Century depression. We just don't see the soup lines. This down turn may stabilize. Recovery will not be a return to where life had been. There are two significant factors making permanent lower living in the U.S. The two factors are *globalization* and *technology.*

Jobs are gone and will not return. We are in a true world economy. We are technologically out-pacing the labor market. Technology is a cause of jobs becoming obsolete. This means education's imperative is to ready people – young, old and older – for this new reality.

Perhaps the responsive education system may be a revised "old-school" model. What would it look like if education had clear focus to these new world paths? Pre-k focusing on nurture and socialization. Kindergarten begins to place reading, writing and arithmetic to the front of the curriculum. Elementary education would spotlight advance fundamentals plus needed technology skills.

Middle-school (aka Junior High School) would then be selecting a specific path of academic – higher education bound, technical – highly skilled training; or service – professional service training.

In the senior year, a student would participate in a dual education prior to graduating. Those on the academic path would also be a first semester college student. A student in technical or service paths would be placed as an intern in their chosen field.

This multiple path of *academic, technological* or *service* would have all the foundational education, career specifics readiness and ultimately a real place to contribute and flourish upon graduation.

Wizard-Type Wonderings

Whatever happened to lotteries underwriting education?

Where exactly does the lottery money go?

At what point in American history did education become a drain, devalued, **and the *bottom of the bucket?***

- What does America produce? Products from America are ____ ? Top three appears to be pharmaceuticals, celebrity/notoriety through entertainment, and gaming – casinos on the stock exchange. Pretty much – drugs, sex and gambling!

- A candidate spends multi-millions of dollars to be elected into a job that lasts a few years and pays relatively little. (Example: 22.6 million on election, approximately 22.18 million out of personal money. Once elected, the salary of $130, 273 was "declined")

- Is it possible that globalization has caused the average company to lower-American labor force to be expendable and become "No Longer Needed vs. Help Wanted"?

- Ages hinge on the focus of the given economy. There have been the Dark Age, Agricultural Age, Industrial Age, Modern Age, etc. What is the best name for this present age?

- Could America become the first "Fourth World Nation"; a once world power now a welfare state? Her people, economy, security and education system, etc. fallen to the bottom of world's bucket.

- What are the implications of candidates paying from personal monies to run a campaign? Is this buying into office? Will only those who can afford to pay for a campaign have a chance of being elected?

- What ever became of the 'four day' work week?

- Will the United States have set a legal requirement for a "living wage" (different than a "minimum age")?

- Who really profits from "Reverse Mortgages"?

- Is education in America reflective of the cultural value and/or status of women and children?

The take-away is this:

- <u>Appreciate</u> - knowledge is power. Do all that is possible to be well informed.

- <u>Acknowledge</u> - economics, finances, and education are intertwined. Education demands a prominent position of high priority.

- <u>Advocate</u> - wherever possible for equitable and just compensation. Current education trend is hindered by having an end result of possibly being among the working poor.

- <u>Address</u> - your personal finances; it is imperative to create your *Living Trust*.

Could they survive?

Have you heard about the next planned "Survivor" show?

Three businessmen and three businesswomen will be dropped in an elementary school classroom for 1 school year. Each business person will be provided with a copy of his/her school district's curriculum, and a class of 20-25 students.

Each business person must complete lesson plans at least 3 days in advance, with annotations for curriculum objectives and modify, organize, or create their materials accordingly. They will be required to teach students, handle misconduct, implement technology, document attendance, write referrals, correct homework, make bulletin boards, compute grades, complete report cards, document benchmarks, communicate with parents, and arrange parent conferences. They must also stand in their doorway between class changes to monitor the hallways.

In addition, they will complete fire drills, tornado drills, and [Code Red] drills for shooting attacks each month.

Each class will have a minimum of five learning-disabled children, three with A.D.H.D., one gifted child, and two who speak limited English. Three students will be labeled with severe behavior problems..

They must attend workshops, faculty meetings, and attend curriculum development meetings. They must also tutor students who are behind and strive to get their 2 non-English speaking children proficient enough to take the state standardized tests.

Each day they must incorporate reading, writing, math, science, and social studies into the program. They must maintain discipline and provide an educationally stimulating environment to motivate students at all times. If all students do not wish to cooperate, work, or learn, the teacher will be held responsible.

The business people will only have access to the public golf course on the weekends, but with their new salary, they will not be able to afford it. There will be no access to vendors who want to take them out to lunch, and lunch will be limited to thirty minutes, which is not counted as part of their work day. The business people will be permitted to use a student restroom, as long as another survival candidate can supervise their class.

If the copier is operable, they may make copies of necessary materials before, or after, school. However, they cannot surpass their monthly limit of copies. The business people must continually advance their education, at their expense, and on their own time.

The winner of this Season of Survivor will be allowed to return to their job.

-Author Unknown

SEMESTER IV
School's Out

A Student Speaks...
Something Worth Fighting For

(Entry level writing from an adult student
in an Alternative School Program)

Something worth fighting for me would be
my business that I am going to open...

I'm hoping soon that I'll have the right
help to give me more incite on the business
industry...I'm still in search of how to raise
money or even have someone to sponsor
me...I'm not giving up on my ideas for
anything because it's not just for money, it's
something I want to do...

I'll like to wake up in the mornings to
get dress up...get ready for myself owned
business...ready to greet my customers. I
know I'm going to have some bad days...I've
learned when something doesn't go your
way, you can't run from your problems, you
have to solve it for yourself... I'm speaking
my business into my future.

Reflections on Students from Sampling

summarized by Ushanda Pauling

(*The exact question from the survey is printed to the left in bold*)

The reflections presented are from the posted survey. It is the intention of **Who's Schooling Who?** to present the responses and reflection as a hint into students input to current issues in education.

A cross section of students were surveyed about their overall school experience and the "pearls of wisdom" they felt they imparted on teachers and professionals within the school as well as pearls that were conveyed to them.

Students were asked what their understanding of education is and how that gets played out in the actual classroom and school community. As with the adults, *we asked that students voice their opinions as to what can be done to change or overhaul our current system to make it better.* In hindsight we could probably add to the question by fleshing it out into parts. For example, we could have asked, "W*hat is the importance of education to parents, school personnel, the local community, society at large, and the individual student;*" all as separate questions. We could have also asked for those separate categories when gathering thoughts about completely overhauling the educational system to make it better for each of those demographics.

The timing of when the survey responses were c ompleted is interesting because they are split between the ending of a school year and the beginning of the school year. We can make some assumptions about how students may feel at the end of the year versus the beginning of the year and how that may change their perspective on education. We can assume those answering at the end of the year carry some fatigue and relief that it is over versus those that are hopeful and possibly anxious about the start of a new school term.

We may also consider that the respondents were all high school aged students. Neither their current grade level nor their "on target grade level" was asked. From this, we could assume they answered with some level of maturity and experience from being in school for several years. We could assume that as seasoned students they possibly have experienced quite a few classroom and school settings, school personnel, and teaching styles.

As a part of the adolescent development process, late adolescence marks a time of deeper moral thinking and greater capacity for abstract thinking and the ability to examine experiences to predict potential effects. We see this in young people that engage in causes and issues that impact them and the world around them. Babyart.org characterizes the cognitive and moral development of middle/ late adolescence by the capacity to discern the underlying principles of various phenomena and apply them to new situations and increased ability (for some) to take another's perspective; can see the bigger societal picture and might value moral principles over laws. (27) Understanding that youth may fall anywhere on the developmental spectrum. At minimum we may glean that the adolescents answering have some level of functioning in these areas.

It is clear from their responses that these young people see education as a valuable tool that provides a bridge to success for them. They openly express that possibilities are opened for them and societal advancements are made as a result of educated people. Respondents went so far as to credit longer school days and more rigorous course work as forces that can mightily contribute to further student success.

What is the importance of education?

In response to the question of the importance of education for them, students responded in a similar fashion of believing education has opened their eyes to see possibilities that could exist for them and also as a key ingredient in their recipe for success. The group attributed education as a source, a tangible resource that could actually help. Advances in technology, medicine, art, and society were noted as products of people being educated. They later attributed education as part of the maturation process and the framework for tangible skills like organization and employment readiness skills. We know that these skills are definitely needed for successful navigation of adulthood.

Another student highlighted that school helps them and is important to their developing concept of their self. Remembering that our respondents are high school aged, we know that their full concept of self is not developed and will occur over time. I do believe it is significant that young people credit the school experience to helping their sense of self take shape. Without spelling it out, that says something other than academics is taking place for them.

What is the trick to being successful in school? And, My school helps me...

All the effort was not placed on the part of the educators. Students also identified they play a role in the success of school and what they are able to take from it. We asked that they tell us some of the tricks they believe helped with being successful in school and progressing from one grade level to another. One might think these responses would be clever, out of the box, maybe even negative; however, this particular sampling kept it simple. Showing up regularly, keeping focused no matter what, wading through massive amounts of information, balance, and time management were the consistent threads in their responses.

Showing up is a powerful concept. It seems simple enough but for some youth in today's world, it can be monstrous. We know all too well that in some of our communities just showing up has been a cumbersome task for students. Truancy programs have been set up across the country based on this very thing. Students' attendance or lack thereof varies for numerous reasons of course, but for many the thought of digging themselves out of the pits of life to come to a place they do not feel is an immediate concern is a chore.

Remember that "*keeping focused no matter what*" is also on the list; right next to showing up. The *"no matter what"* part of the response signifies that students have things happen in their lives that are significant. The significance of these occurrences may differ among individuals, but it could be the source of academic decline, distraction and decreased attendance. If you have been around a school campus for any length of time, you begin to notice times where students all but disappear mentally, emotionally, and ultimately physically. The responses from this sampling provide a great reminder to parents, educators, administrators, mentors and the like, to encourage these two areas in tandem.

Checking in with the students in our lives about what they may be going through, providing support, and encouragement to stay focused on scholastic achievement; so that showing up doesn't become an issue can be of great assistance to a student's overall success. There are so many students just floating and no one even knows they are missing or why.

It was not a part of this samplings response to include parents as part of their repertoire for success, but they did acknowledge their involvement when asked about how parents can be involved in schools more. We can assume they did not think about it, but a more factual rationale may be what we know about adolescent development. If we had surveyed elementary level youth, the responses would have probably listed parents first. Developmentally it makes sense that their responses are such. Middle and late adolescence is marked by increased independence and autonomy. (27)

What ways can parents get more involved in schools?

For this sampling they fall right in the midst of this developmental period. Parents are an after thought or an "as needed" resource, not an essential factor during this time period. The responses about parents involvement in their school experience is connected to other parents not them as a student necessarily. It is the idea of insurance; knowing that it's there but only calling it forth when needed. Students listed:

- Join the P.T.A and meet other parents.
- Chaperone events.
- Be there for help with harder classes, but back off some times and give the student a break.
- Check on their grade/ overall progress.

Things I teach my teachers.

We asked students for some suggestions for teachers and education decision makers that could improve the system of education. This was another area that provided some insight to students' actual thoughts about education. For some readers, it may come as a surprise that students are actually thinking about education and not just going through the process.

Another developmental marking that came through in their comments was a desire to have competent educators that are aware of diversity and have some practical skills in teaching diverse groups of students. Their definition of diversity was in personality and learning styles. Again, maybe shocking for some readers to believe that students are actively thinking along these lines, but it is plainly written out.

One student reports they find it helpful when teachers make the classroom fun and can lighten up. They stated they are able to learn more on those days and can retain that information better. As adults this is played out in the workforce. We thrive in our work and report much higher job satisfaction when we are in pleasant environments that allow for fun. Why wouldn't this be true for students? An environment that you have to be in for such a large portion of the day should provide some level enjoyment, shouldn't it?

Seems simple yet insightful, to recognize that educators be able to teach in a number of different school settings to a number of different personalities and learning styles, is an asset to the learning environment. We know there is more than one learning style and that most of us have a particular style that optimizes the information we can take in and process for understanding. However, when you take a snapshot in to many classrooms of today, you find one dimensional teaching methods. That is true from the youngest of learners up through higher education. I was in graduate school a few years back, and there were instructors that literally lectured for hours. In this day and age, full fledge lecturing is almost prehistoric. This is another area where funding and economics come into play because all students in all classrooms are not given the same opportunity to have instruction in multiple dimensions. I do not know if the college curriculum or the supplemental continuing teacher education courses are the place to infuse it, but teachers need more time and instruction on how to deliver material in more than one learning style.

How could the education system be completely overhauled?

When given the temporary option to become the wizard and completely overhaul the system of education, responses were incredibly insightful in areas most adults wouldn't give youth credit for even having awareness of. They suggested something be done about who is hired to teach them. They didn't say hiring genius level educators or master teachers; it was very simply put; *"hire teachers that care."* Looking at their previous statements about having teachers that can instruct to various learning styles and personalities, goes right in line with this thought of having teachers that care.

We have all had experiences with teachers through

direct contact, observation, or report from another person, that didn't seem to really like youth and certainly wouldn't ever be accused of caring about them. Those types of teachers sour the field, taint the educational experience, and force youth out of the school doors in droves! You would think anyone willing to get in to the field would have an incredible love and passion for youth and education; sadly there are people who enter the field for very different reasons. There is a correlation to that in one of the other responses given, and that is to either get rid of or drastically revamp the seniority scale.

One respondent noted their school lost a teaching unit which translated in to the loss of a great teacher. The loss of the great teacher meant students were divided out to other classrooms. As luck would have it, this respondent ended up with the lack-luster burned out, senior teacher that could've cared less if the students learned anything. Has anyone ever thought about conducting teacher evaluations in schools like they do in colleges at the end of a semester and truly having that information carry weight that affected teachers' employment? From this response it screams that students feel their voice is missing when it comes to who instructs them.

In all my experience in working with youth, I continue to be affirmed and delighted that they are thinking and assessing, even when adults aren't expecting them to or caring if it happens. From this sampling, the realization was noted that the system we currently subject our youth to and have gone along with year after year, may in fact need some major restructuring. This sampling suggested, "*Start from scratch, lose the idea that education be a benefit to big government, and ask the true parties involved what they want and deliver it!*" Wow! That says so much so simply. They listed, ask students, parents, teachers, faculty, and the public their opinions about what they want from education and recreate the system to meet those needs and expectations. There is no reason to comment further on that other than to say, "Can you hear me now?"

Describe ways that you "school" the adults in your school.

Conversely, we asked students how they *"school"* the teachers and other adults at their school. They have already pointed out things are being taught regularly in schools that have nothing to do with academic subject matter. This group of students believe they remind adults and teachers some of the basics of human interaction like looking up when walking down the hallways and saying hello to them or other students when passing by. One of the daily common courtesies is addressing people by name and treating them with dignity and respect. I was in a meeting and someone told the story of a seasoned teacher conducting an entire class period without using any students names, pointing her finger, and making threats to remove children from the classroom as opposed to redirecting or managing behavior in a more productive manner.

As an aside, in some of the responses, there is an absence of recognizing the power of a mentor. This is interesting because we have research that speaks to the value of positive adult role models and mentors in the lives of youth. However, youth themselves may not always realize the significance of having such a figure. In reading the responses from this sampling, that became glaringly obvious to me. From their responses about tricks to school success, that seemed like the perfect place to add a mentor. Remember, they pointed out showing up and staying focused? Who better to help than a mentor to fill in the gap for parents and teachers?

What do state standardized tests say about the education of students?

We couldn't discuss education with real students and not ask them about their thoughts on standardized testing and what that reveals about their education. I must admit, I was a little surprised at the responses and that they didn't totally bash testing or speak very low of its point and purpose.

Sometimes when I visit schools, especially during testing season, there is a general feel of tension and anxiety; sometimes verbalized in complete dislike for that time of year and what the test results might actually mean. It is no surprise this particular sampling looked at testing a bit more objectively and balanced and their responses acknowledged that testing is not a complete waste of their time. They seem to understand the design of the test is to serve as a guide to ensure that students receive consistent education in schools.

The statement of helping to better the education schools give acknowledges that some schools are doing well and some are falling below on the quality of education their student body receives. There is also a statement of accountability that isn't spoken outright but can be inferred. If testing is done to help better what some schools are offering to their students, then it stands to reason that this sampling recognizes schools are giving less than what's needed to be accountable to the same degree. It was not asked for them to assess the quality of education that they receive so we do not know what type of schools this sampling attends (neighborhood, suburban, city, rural, etc.), the school grade, nor their quality of educators, and makeup of the general student body. When reviewing these responses I gather a sense this group does place some value on standardize tests ability to measure what they know and to have something that is equal across the board. Again, recognizing the test provides some guarantee that equal education and information sharing is taking place.

One of the respondents did not feel as warm towards testing as the others. This particular respondent felt the test actually told very little about a student's education. It was stated that, "The average student is not a good test taker and to base important decisions about their education upon test scores is unfair and inaccurate." They didn't elaborate on what exactly important decisions entails, but here in the state of Florida, standardize tests determine things like promotion to the next grade level, educational track during school, graduation from high school, and more.

The point of all students not being good test takers is a great one. As a student, I personally was never a good test taker and my scores always had to be evaluated against my regular classroom work and grade point average. My percentile scoring was never particularly high and it was shown year after year that the results were really not an accurate measure of what I knew. Fortunately, I was in school during a time that the scores didn't carry the same weight as they do today. So I personally can relate to the respondent not wanting the school to be judge and jury about the status of one's education. In today's system I may very well be one of those students not promoted or not able to receive my high school diploma because there was a portion of the test that I could not pass. Think about the poor test takers. For most of us who are, we already know we do not do well on those kinds of tests. So we enter an environment already slightly defeated in our attitude about the test. Tack on that testing brings its own anxiety because it forces students to recall information under pressure (time and understanding of the impact of their score). The combination of these things doesn't exactly create an environment for best efforts to come forth. Many schools have implemented prep strategies and coaching for students identified as having a potentially difficult time taking tests. Other measures have been introduced to defray or erase any potential hindrances to students testing performance. While they are great efforts and do have an impact, the fact still remains that some students just cannot perform to their maximum potential in this type of scenario. In reviewing and summarizing the responses from this sampling, it reveals a few more questions and sheds some light on a few observations.

Please note the theme from students is that they do value and view education as a critical part of their lives and one that they feel could be an absolute benefit as they grow and mature. While adults might feel the most important part of education is the academic piece, students see things a little differently. For this sampling, it was made clear that the relational and social aspects of education were the foundational pieces for success along with the academic pieces. This reveals there is a need to gain agreement among the involved parties on what education is and what the goals are.

Having expectations set right from the beginning could better chart the course of education in a different direction as we look to address other issues. The issues of money and funding to schools shows not only do teachers verbalize and share some of their opinions about money with students, but the funding cuts and money shortages within schools is most certainly felt by the student body. As we look to address issues of education, it is obvious that student's voices be not only solicited but heard and factored into the overall decision making process.

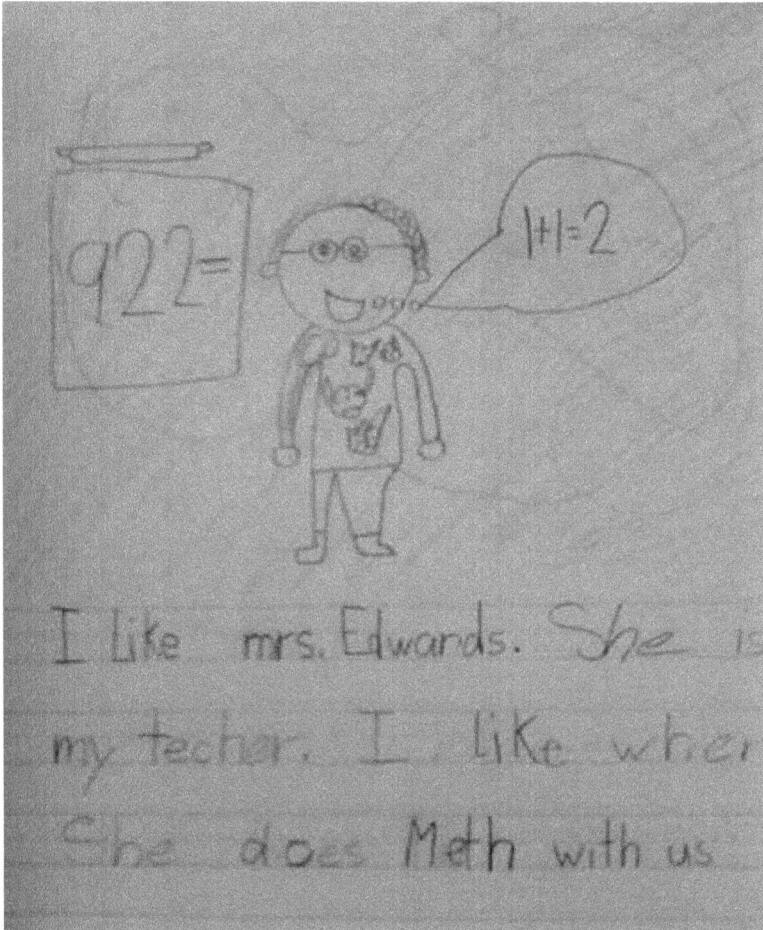

(28)

Meth Teacher? Little Kid Makes Hilarious Misspelling

What a difference one letter makes

www.huffingtonpost.com

Reflections on Teachers from Sampling

summarized by Veronica Blakely

(*The exact question from the survey is printed to the left in bold*)

What is the importance of education?

Overall agreement that education is important.

- The respondents felt that education is the foundation of everything we do and without it we are nothing.

- A consensus noted the importance of a quality education allowing students to reach their fullest potential and ultimately lead to success.

- An education is needed to ensure students become effective members of our society.

My thoughts about our current education system and how it can be improved.

This question sparked some very passionate and deep felt responses.

- Noted frustration with the No Child Left Behind Act (NCLB) that has placed additional burdens on the classroom environment for students and teachers.

- Teacher morale is low and so is the pay.

- Budget cuts have put a strain on a system already on the brink of a breakdown.

- Lots of inequality in the system for teachers and students which has led to apathy for all. Some teachers do not teach as they should and some students do not seem to want to learn.

How does the school(s) your child(ren) attend benefit parents?	Similar responses of school being a safe haven for students.

- Schools reinforce manners and social skills students may or may not have learned at home.
- Parents can feel assured that their child is receiving the proper care and instruction for their education.
- Schools act like a second home for students offering food, shelter, and transportation.

What is the trick to being successful in school?	Straight forward and direct responses to this question.

- Building relationships with students, parents, teachers, and the community.
- Sharing, being part of the solution and not part of the problem.
- Parental involvement.

What do state standardized tests say about the education of students?	Respondents had a lot to say about this topic.

- Not an advocate of these tests.
- Not sure students are meeting the standards.
- Teachers are teaching to the test instead of teaching students how to learn.
- It is a snap shot of what students can do one day out of the year.
- These tests do not measure all aspects of what a student learns.
- The test measure students against each other and not on what each individual is able to do.

At school, my child(ren) learn...

A consensus about life skills.

- Lifelong skills and respect.
- The fundamentals of life.
- The basics of reading, writing, and arithmetic.
- Survival skills for life.

What ways can parents get more involved in school?

Responses focused on parents taking part in some way as long as they were present for their child(ren).

- Attend conferences to check student's status.
- Volunteer or be a mentor.
- Be supportive of the teacher
- Be available by phone or email so that the teacher can contact the parent.
- Support all school activities.
- Be present or ask some else to stand in for you.

How can the education system be overhauled?

Lots of good advice offered.

- Get better leadership.
- Can't overhaul the entire system; get better policies.
- Increase teacher salaries.
- Legislators say they care about our youth, but they do not put money where it is needed.
- Put money back into the budget for better schools for teachers and students.

I have gotten "schooled" by students in the following way(s).

Most responses related to the bond students and teachers make.

- Students taught the teacher how to listen.

- Students taught teachers that students want as well as need respect guardian.

- Students taught teachers about technology and their choice of music.

OPINIONS

On the first day of school, a first-grader handed his teacher a note from his mother. The note read, 'The opinions expressed by this child are not necessarily those of his parents.'

-Unknown

Reflections on Parents and Guardians from Sampling

summarized by Lynnette Stallworth
(The exact question from the survey is printed to the left in bold)

The reflection presented is based the posted survey. It is the intention of **Who's Schooling Who?** to present the responses and reflection as a hint into parents and guardians input to the current education issue.

Most children were in elementary and middle school. The respondents had an average of two to three students. There were nine specific questions or statements.

What is the importance of education?

As is often said, "Everyone is entitled to their own opinion!" In this case, everyone without exception had the same opinion. The expressed opinion was that education is important.

There were different ways to say the same thing. In general the sentiment was education is important to one's self and society. A strong statement was the importance of education is a, "lifetime success". Another response which supports education's importance for the nation was expressed in this phrase – "lifeblood of our country."

Further conversation might be whether the responses were anticipated or unconventional or even deeply reflective.

My thoughts about our current education system and how it can be improved.

This statement brought everyone "to their feet!" More than any other question or statement this one singularly garnered the most responses.

If charted it would look something like this:

Current Education System	How it can Improve
Opted/Out – child in private school	Need more discipline
Completely corrupted	Teach current, make relevant
Lack of flexibility	Curriculum to hold student attention
Lack of parental involvement	Penalty for non-parental involvement
Teachers stress passed onto children	Teaching to learn not to pass tests
Think education system is good.	No more half days
Parents fail kids	

While the responses were highly engaging, the critical point could be missed. What parents/ guardians have to say is a lot/ a lot, but that they have a lot/ a lot to say is central. The clarity and volume indicates parents are eager to participate in this emerging effort to transform education. Has anyone asked parents/guardians? Has anyone heard their voices?

I am involved in my child(ren)'s education by......

The response to this statement is best viewed as "every little bit helps the cause." There is the "highly involved parents/guardian," "medium-involved," "barely-involved," "cheerleader-involved" and the "call-it-in-involved." Those were our respondents. As known all too well, there are the complete no-show parents/guardians. It then is no surprise they were not represented.

The "call-it-in involved" parents/guardians are just that; they keep contact by way of the phone and by electronic means like texting or email.

The "cheerleader involved" parents/guardians are there to give "emotional support and encouragement" as their primary involvement in their child's education.

The "barely involved" shown as, "my husband has always been lead role with homework, projects..." This group may also be seen as basic, very basic-involvement which was shared as, '...keep my child well fed, well dressed and on a regular routine for school...'

The "medium involved" attempts to participate either in broad-strokes or specific activity. They are likely to volunteer and be in regular contact with the teacher.

The "highly involved" parent/guardian is in overdrive. This parent/guardian wants to "send the message; this child has people in her corner and are her advocate." Another response sheds light on this type of guardian involvement as said, "being classroom mom, going to parent-teacher conferences, talking with teacher, volunteering for functions." Rosalind Wiseman vividly outlines this in the book, *Queen Bee Moms and Kingpin Dads.* (29)

Every parent/guardian is to be acknowledged for their contribution to their students' educational success. The variety of home structures and dynamics are not revealed here.

How does the school(s) your child(ren) attend benefit parents/ guardians?

"When my partner died I called the school to notify them my daughter would not be in school for several days. The assistant principal knew him by name – I did not know she knew him, this is the type of personalization that's important. Invest in the child, her family and you have a recipe for success."

A most moving testimony of how your child's school benefits parents. This is how schools were in days far gone and perhaps how school could be again.

The above is noteworthy to stand alone. Other responses held the relationship of school and home in high regard.

The benefits included; "keeps us in THE KNOW, networking with other parents, keeping children safe from violence gives parents ease to be about their day, serves as socializing base for child which sometimes becomes our friends, after school extended day program a huge help and fundraising events help defray cost for families."

Who knew? Schools help families. Families support schools. This makes a cyclical relationship otherwise known as a community of mutual satisfaction.

What is the trick to being successful in school?

Fascinating! It's one perspective to view each response separately. It's quite different viewing all responses together. It is as if having many pieces presents and spreads out a cohesive picture.

Currently, in the public discourse a successful school is weighted on the teachers. In conversations success is about quality teachers. The many pieces on their own hold teachers as key to school success. Here are parent's/guardian's pieces of the puzzle.

Parent's/Guardian's without exception place school success on themselves! They have to be helped to see their own collective responses. Right now they know their separate response. "Home life stable, regular contact with school" and "Instill importance of education, self-motivation and good behavior" were the cornerstone of parent/guardian responses.

The next level of success was responses of parents "full participation – class and extra-curriculum." Added to this level was "reinforcing rules."

And then the crowning piece, that last puzzle piece of "collaborating effort with child, teacher, principal and parent."

At school my child(ren) learns…

Keep in mind the statement. The interpretation for what the child "learned" is solely in the control of the parent/guardian. The responses were lack-luster. There was virtually no enthusiasm in the responses. What might this imply? Does it correlate with parent's/guardian's statements of need for teaching "relevant" curriculum, "making learning fun" or "keeping student's attention?"

The responses fit comfortably into one of four categories. The offered categories are:

Academic
- Academic basics.
- Reading, math & science.
- Spanish.

Social

- How to appropriately interact with peers.
- To be responsible and accountable.

Life Lessons

- See how other families live – not always as good as they live; and sometimes better.
- Time management and problem-solving.
- Finding their place in society.

Miscellaneous

- Taking tests.
- What is required by the State? Not really what the teacher could really teach our children."

What do state standard-ized tests say about the education of students?

The question was similar to a Supreme Court decision. The majority of "the court" (respondents) were in the negative.

Don't believe it's a true picture of a child's education.

- Never agreed with this way of testing.
- Creates unnecessary stress.
- Not every student tests well, doesn't mean student did not or cannot learn.
- Son transferred to a different state he had a lot to catch up on.
- It's not working.
- Math plays too big a role on tests.

The minority or "descending" respondents held positive view of standardized tests.

- My son scored higher...(tests) say he is in the right place.
- The student can perform under pressure.
- Shows where the gaps are.

What ways can parents/guardians get more "involved" in schools?

The respondent's in this survey appear to have a substantial understanding of being involved in schools in order to have a good learning experience. By-in-large their responses were all the usual heard of, asked for, and spoken about in education discussions.

There were a few that would make one sit-up and pay attention; these are important responses.

1. Parents/Guardians who are already involved should support letting teachers teach with passion.

2. Ask the teacher what they need to do their job and help them to be heard by local and national government.

3. Meet the child's friends and their parents/guardians.

4. Make sure the teacher associates you with your child not someone else's.

5. There are too many ways to list, but one way is to not be afraid to say NO! Children need to know that NO is one word that shows LOVE.

6. Become a teacher.

It is time to have a forum for parents/guardians to talk, share and develop their best input to bringing remedy to this education crisis.

There is one curious issue not mentioned by parents/guardians anywhere in the sampling. No one commented on the manner in which students are educated. There was no mention of how we actually educate. This may be indicative of being conditioned or not critically analyzing what's happening beneath the surface of what they experience.

The simple foundational question of, "How is curricula developed?" needs attention. It may have been alluded to earlier, but needs to be fully defined and addressed.

I have gotten "schooled" by students in the following way(s).

It turns out the "Book Project" has been "schooled". For the most part, the statement was not understood. We appreciate the respondent's candor in saying, "sorry, do not understand the question."

What they did say was their child(ren) "schooled" them on current trends and new technology. On a deeper level there was, "learning about who I am through different encounters with them."

My Experience

*An interview with Danon Ferguson, an inner city teacher of 15
plus years in middle school education.*
with Lynnette Stallworth

Danon, how is it that you became a teacher?

A number of things happened. My parents were very involved with
education.

I did an internship at the University of Michigan with a program called
King Chavez Parks (KCP). The purpose of the program was to encourage
young at-risk inner city kids; which spoke to my heart more so than my
field of study in engineering.

I was more fortunate than most growing up. My father had and has now
a significant influence in my life. He taught me academic achievement is
as important as giving back to others. My father is an excellent example of
being a man and a father.

I attended a then highly ranked suburban public school and in recent years
I've heard things have changed at my high school. What students come to
education with is much less.

Ultimately, education chose me and I have given it the last 15 years of my
life.

What is your view of education now?

To me, there are two separate school systems in the United States. There is
mainstream and Third World. Mainstream is failing and Third World has
failed! Third World schools are predominantly in low income communities.
Third World schools are colorblind; there are black, brown, white, and
yellow students in these schools.

From your vantage point, "who's schooling who?"

That's a really good question... I used to think the teacher was "schooling"
students and administration. My reality has changed. I've been "schooled"
by students a lot. The most important lesson students have taught me

(especially those at risk in the inner city) is not to get caught up in my own expectations. That lesson was big in Highland Park along with setting my expectations aside. I've been shown 'don't be fooled by what you think you see'. I've had students who put in an acceptable appearance. They may look groomed and properly dressed only to find out their living conditions are awful!

Students may be homeless or rearing siblings. I've been "schooled" to make the effort to become aware of a student's true living conditions. Sometimes the lessons students teach go beyond the physical or outer issues. They teach matters of the human spirit. More recently, I have been shocked by the resolve students have despite their circumstances!

Another "who's schooling who?" on the top of my list would be learn to make sure as a teacher I build rapport before working on assumptions. I've been well 'schooled' that a teacher can't treat all students the same.

As for administration well...that's a whole different story. I used to think telling administration the facts of the situation would lead to a possibility of resolution of the situation. Administration has 'schooled' me, that telling them means little. This is a major frustration felt by teachers and seen by students.

Would you share in your opinion of some good teaching techniques?

Sure, give students responsibility for their classrooms. Start in the beginning of the school year when putting physical items, posters, etc. in the room. Allow them to pick and choose and suggest how the room, their rooms, will be arranged.

Develop opportunities for students to participate.

Give them ownership. They are not just "tenants". Help students make it their classroom...it's not exclusively the teacher's.

Then there's the matter of being consistent and fair. Even if they don't like what you are directing they will work with you as long as they can see and experience that you're being fair and consistent.

I hold being organized as more than helpful. It will make the day go better for teaching and for the student. Being organized also lets students know that you respect them and their time. Organization also sets a very good example for future work ethic.

And lastly, I would highly encourage a teacher to use a variety of instructing methods like small groups or discussion teams. There is also reflective writing. I encourage mixing it up to keep the students attentive.

Earlier you mentioned school administration. I'm wondering in general, what ways has school administration added to or taken away from successful learning?

Administration plays a tremendous role in learning success and academic achievement. Administration is the leadership in education. The leadership can make or break the school setting. When administration is genuinely caring of students and teachers and staff then there is the first leg up for success. When you're not appreciated and shown respect that is a problem.

An example is an administrator requiring teachers, staff and students to be punctual, yet they are notoriously late and offer no apology. A good administrator leads by example…"does what they expect others to do; not do as they say…"

Administrators must have a vision and the ability to share the vision with others if the school is to be successful. The difference in adding to the success of a school is an administrator who finds ways to empower teachers, students and staff. If there is no empowerment, no vision, power, and leadership skills, then the administrator detracts from every effort made for successful education. I sometimes wonder if administrators understand the difference between managing and leading!

If you could what would be some of the changes you would make in the immediate to the current school system?

First, I believe we should be in <u>school year round</u>. The concept of "summer vacation" is erroneous. All students need more time in the classroom particularly inner-city youngsters. They have no time to waste!

Next is the issue of higher education as a universal goal. Definitely an admirable goal, but it's not necessarily for everybody. We don't put enough emphasis on making connections on where the student is now and how to help the student make a living for the future. We need more vocational training. The purest from academics standpoint need not look down on plumbers and electricians and folks that help with all kinds of services. A college career is not always mandatory.

If more <u>vocational training</u> were offered to meet the students where they are and where their hopes and dreams are taking them, perhaps the drop-out rate may be lower.

Another immediate change in current education I would suggest is <u>mentoring</u>. Mentoring is an intensive way by all and any who are stakeholders. This means those folks in the community organizations like Elks, NAACP, fraternities, sororities, businesses, local government, everyone who has a stake in education. These groups can connect with the school. The school can be the hub where would be the one-to-one exposure to different worldviews. As mentors they would learn to listen to discern and to develop career goals with the students. Perhaps the organization of these various stakeholders could be done through/by chamber of commerce and/or places of worship. The point is it is needed...now!

Right now it appears that parents are not fulfilling their role entirely. I would offer that in the immediate future there must be a way created to require support and participation from parents. Families having interest in their children have better outcomes. We all know this. Now is time to <u>require it not just request parent participation.</u>

These recommendations grow from my fundamental belief that students need a high level of care and concern. They may not have concern for themselves right now but eventually they will! It may not be when you, I or the teacher sees it. There will come a time when the student will say, "...Mr. Ferguson I'm headed to college or a training program because of what you taught me..." Keep in mind, a student does not stay where they are!

A Support Staff's Perspective: "The Lunch Lady"

by Lynnette Stallworth

Who would believe I'd ever be "The Lunch Lady!?" Life does offer twists and unexpected turns. In this case the winding road led me to an ideal position.

The hours were my cup-of-tea; on the job 9:45 AM to 1:45 PM. The only paperwork was filling out daily sheets. No take home work; with the exception of my volunteering to wash rags. This way I knew they were fresh and well sanitized.

There was parking at the door, less than a 20 minute commute, school t-shirt, complimentary lunch each day and the delight of being in the energy of 21st Century youngsters. Little did I know the job would become Grammy training grounds as my son and daughter-in-law were first time expectant parents. Nor did I know being "The Lunch Lady" in a suburban elementary school would supply a boat-load of experiences giving me a new view on education.

Who knew the cafeteria is without a doubt <u>The Best Seat In The School</u>! The cafeteria is comparable to the kitchen at home. The cafeteria is the heart, pulse, gathering place every day at school. From this location one encounters on a daily basis teachers, administrators, parents, support staff, vendors, guest and students. The student body does not go to the office every day. The student body goes to the cafeteria every day.

Plus there was the bonus feature of interacting with teachers as they "handed" their class over to the lunch lady and "retrieved" them from me.

Imagine this serendipitous opportunity to actively observe undetected yet in full view approximately 800 suburban elementary students pre-K (4 years old) to fifth grade (11 to 12 years old), Monday through Friday for three uninterrupted hours.

The school facility-campus was less than five years old and boasts being a premier school in the district. At times I felt like a spy or like the persons on the TV program "Under Cover Boss."

Being the "lunch lady" was a gold mine. But wait a minute even gold mines require serious 'put your back into it' labor! Thank goodness I did not have to mind the entire room alone, that only happened on a few occasions. There were two sides of the cafeteria with a "lunch lady" for each side. I was responsible for 12 tables (each numbered) seating 12 students (assigned seating) at each. There were four lunch periods, beginning with fifth-graders.

Training and Learning

At first glance the arrangement appears reasonable. My training consisted of logistics with positioning trash barrels, the water bucket and table wiping. There was instruction on the rules which were posted in various places on the walls around the cafeteria. The rules were emphasized by the person training me. Missing from training was follow up on CPR or any other safety emergency operations. What I did not get, to my surprise, was an overall orientation including meeting faculty, principal, assistant principal, support staff such as custodian, bus drivers, or Parent- Teacher Association rep (PTA); nor was there a map given showing the location of the nurses office, bathrooms, or emergency exit or evacuation plan.

Learning to be "The Lunch Lady" began for real when a woman's voice from the kitchen bellowed loud, long, and clear, "They're here!" I was now officially "The Lunch Lady." It would take Erma Bombeck or Bill Cosby to describe this "game-on" scene. From that cry of "they're here!" until a suddenly empty great hall it was non-stop motion. The sound level was literally deafening. The noise of hundreds of kids in closed quarters requires, from time to time, the signal for quiet. When the raising of hands did not work the whistle had to be blown. My colleague had the one whistle; which meant she and I had to use a lot of eye contact. Considering the chaotic state of the cafeteria coupled with one person to maintain safety and personal security it is a wonder there was not any "bad outcomes". Think about it; one person supervising 100 kids, while cleaning, is expected to insure each child's safety.

There are officials on a football field. The football officials are supervising eleven (11) players not cleaning and expected to watch for rule infractions only. The "Lunch Lady" is a 1 to 100 give or take ration. What might that comparison imply? Perhaps what the football player is doing has more value than what the student is doing? Let's take it to a more serious level or similar scenario happens for school bus drivers. One driver with many children is 100% responsible for everyone's safety. As if driving a rectangular box on six wheels is not enough.

I learned to prioritize giving attention to raised hands first <u>then</u> clearing and cleaning a table. What do you suppose are options for school bus drivers? What does the supervision/ supervisor ratio say about our cultural values?

Incidents

As anyone might imagine there were more incidents than can be counted. Each incident had its own lesson. Not every lesson has been fully digested or discerned. A few incidents can be bundled as to their lessons. For instance, there were repeatedly students entering, looking into my face and not speaking. Over and over a student would misbehave and robotically say, "…it was an accident, I'm sorry…!" These incidents suggest need for teaching socialization skills, manners, and taking responsibility. The student is teaching us they will say what we adults want to hear. These two incidents may also be students tugging at adults looking for ways to be more genuinely and humanly connected. It may be that this was an adaptation to the culture of this particular school; a "premier school".

Of course there were incidents that were in and of themselves memorable and powerful such as "The Fight".

The Fight

First day of school was a Tuesday. The day went well as did the Wednesday, Thursday and Friday that followed. We were getting acquainted with one another as well as the cafeteria routine. After a refreshing weekend it was Monday, 5th day of the new school year. Arriving with my new apron (pockets for "silverware" and ketchup) and ever increasing confidence as "The Lunch Lady" I entered this, my other world.

"They're here!" and we were off and moving. Tables 13-24 were all smiled at and greeted. All is well! "There's a fight….they're fighting!" came the shouts from my side of the cafeteria. Spinning around I saw nothing. Then in the very middle large center aisle that divides the room on the floor next to table 19 was a small (4'11") framed eye-glassed fifth grade boy flat on his back. Straddled over him was a slim almost lanky (5'5") fifth grade boy with his left hand on the smaller kid's chest and his right hand tightly fisted raising well behind his head hitting the eye-glassed classmate over and over. Both lunch ladies ran over to the scene. Teachers from the teacher's room came and the boys were pulled apart. Out of nowhere the assistant principal, a former athlete (strapping, 6'3" – large guy) appeared. He had the boys by the back of their collars.

My first duty was to reassure students and help calm them. They wanted to tell what they saw and heard.

Fast forward to the next day, Tuesday. I was mouth-dropped shocked to see both boys back in the cafeteria at the same table, my table 19! I had never ever personally witnessed such physical violence in my life. How was I to treat these guys? The students at table 19 were one little girl who was shaking like a leaf just yesterday. What do I do? What do I do? No one – not the teacher or assistant principal ever said a word. I thought for sure they both were suspended or at least not allowed to come to school for a day. The week passed. I kept an eye on table 19 and never turned my back on the two boys. The teacher at "delivery" and "retrieval" asked how lunch time was.

It was into the fourth week of school when the assistant principal called me and my colleague lunch lady into his office. This agenda was singular; "careful not to put students (table or room) on silent lunch as students will tell parents and then parents would get upset and he would have a headache!" Honest to goodness that was it. There were no thanks for your work, no asking if we had anything to discuss.

I tried to keep my mouth shout, but before I knew it, I was asking about the fight. His response was, "…spoke with parents….everything is okay…!" This troubled me greatly. I selectively told the incident to friends who are educators. Then there it was – Bingo – this particular educator explained,

"It's the count." I heard, "It's the count, stupid." Simply put; until the official stats for the day that measures how many students are in attendance, nobody gets put out no matter what. "The count" is the key to the formula of how much money ($$$) your school district gets for the year. Fewer students equal fewer dollars. End of story....or is it? When was the last time you inquired about the dollar value for each student in your district? Do you know when "the count day" is in your district? Sounds to me that is when schooling truly begins.

The Singer

The last group in for lunch is a smaller number which means the possibility of a slower pace and more interaction with the students. They are also the most hungry so don't talk with them until they are fed.

We sometimes did things across the room. On this particular afternoon my side had had "open mic" for anyone who wanted to sing or dance. "The Lunch Lady" became the emcee. It was a great time. From across the room my colleague said a particular student had a song he wanted to sing. My side tables 13 and 14 said "ok let's hear him…!" in a rather ho-hum way. The student, a fourth grader (9 or 10 years old) faintly freckled checks with a bounce in his step and his head looking down was invited by the MC to stand center aisle. He cleared his throat, kicked his foot to open stance lifted his head and sang. Did I say "sang?" I meant S-A-N-G!! It was a country song. He sang from his toes, his heart, and his gifted voice "Proud to be an American" by Lee Greenwood. His applause was so spontaneous, enthusiastic, genuine and loud. The teachers remaining in the teacher's lunchroom and kitchen staff doing kitchen work came running with concern asking "What happened, what's the matter?" Then they heard and saw and we all were lifted that day by the student singer.

Lockdown

Lockdown! Okay, here is another learning experience on the job because I certainly wasn't trained about "lockdowns." To this day I still don't know all the levels but experienced two. One is "full-lockdown;" stay where you are until given clearance. The other I experienced was a "modified-lockdown;" movement in specific area for specific purpose is allowed.

There was another lockdown that was more like a "rumored-lockdown!" That's when teachers are not sure and adults are whispering, "I think there's a lockdown….my class let's go….!

That's the best I can state as the administration never spoke about the lockdowns before, during or after. The kitchen staff had the best means of knowing off campus information as there was a radio in the back at one of the lockdowns (the full-lockdown). A parent was having lunch with his child. I saw him on his cell phone and asked him if he would go online to a local news site to get any information. No information came. Now keep in mind "The Lunch Lady" is responsible for students not being told or knowing what is the reason behind the lockdown. All I knew was the principal came over the loudspeaker and said "we are in a lockdown…stay put." Immediately the two custodians locked all doors to the cafeteria. These lockdowns were not a good experience. Quite honestly I felt pure resentment. I was expected to take care of these little ones without knowledge and aid. It was one thing to have external danger – the primary reason for the lockdown, but internal danger from the lack of communication from the principal.

The icing on the cake was being locked-up (I mean locked-down) with more than 100 pre-k and kindergarteners (4 and 5 year olds) who had just ingested pounds of sugar. This was a time to "grin and bear it." Did I mention teachers came out once and went back into the teacher's lunchroom?

The modified lockdown I discovered, after getting home, was due to a police hunt in the subdivision where the school is located. There had been a helicopter over the campus. That was the same lockdown where the custodian locked the cafeteria doors and a teacher with her class decided to return. They were locked-out of the lockdown. "The Lunch Lady" happened to hear her tapping and see her face in the window. I let them in. Was I supposed to?

So how safe are children at school? Are the external threats made worse by the ineptness within the facility management?

Table Conversation

Like a server in any restaurant, conversations being had by guests are easily heard. The difference is as "The Lunch Lady" I am supposed to listen, monitor and if necessary take some action. For the most part every table wants you to be part of the conversation. They want you to settle a debate, give input, deliver a message to another table, encourage someone, push your buttons, and play a riddle game or the tag!

I had been told by a teacher that after the December break is when you see measurable maturity in a student. That stayed in my mind and proved true. Table 17 had been an antsy group; particularly the foursome toward the kitchen-end of the table. They were always well-mannered, just silly and wanted my attention. It was not surprising when they waved me over the first full week back in January.

Because I truly enjoyed the students it was rarely, if ever a problem to respond as requested. As I approached there were "four" ready for the world faces looking up at me. Their eyes at age 9 and 10 still carry that star like light. They wanted me to join in their conversation. "Who are you most like? Your Mom or Dad?" I was floored, tickled and drawn in at once. Who are these people? They are not the sillies of 2 ½ weeks ago. I hung back with my response. Admittedly a bit suspicious, but more wanting them to continue their very adult, sophisticated, engaging conversation amongst themselves.

I asked them who they thought they were like. With such calm, self-confidence and new self-awareness they each shared who they were most like and why. Wow! This is that after winter break maturity. The teacher knew and was right. Could it be some teachers are "Yoda's" (the Star Wars character filled with knowing, patience, understanding and wisdom - who want only to give and send you to do)?

The table conversation with the now matured foursome continued and was our "inside" sharing from then on.

Drunk Parents

Did the definition of "Yoda" in Table Conversation quickly bring to mind any parents or guardians you know? You yourself may well fit the definition. Bless you and all the others in that "Yoda" category. The next incident is of parents on quite the other end of the spectrum.

It was kindergartens lunch period. This was table 22 at the auditorium stage end of the cafeteria. They were the extremely shy youngsters. They were quiet, quiet. I always made it a point to greet them early and check on them. While standing in the middle of my half of the room I noticed a woman about 35; dirty blond stringy hair. She was about 5'6" and size three wearing plain beige pedal-pushers and a non-descript white cotton top. As she stood near the stage she began to scan the room. She leaned forward and took two steps that appeared staggered. I saw in her hand a McDonald's™ bag. It was not out of the ordinary for parents to bring McDonalds™, Subway™, or even a special ethnic food for their student and/ or class. I also noticed she did not have a visitors name tag on. My antenna went up. Our eyes fell on each other and she smiled a bit and staggered towards me. By the time she was two feet away the odor of alcohol wreaked unmistakably. This was another situation that was not part of our training. This is a parent. Parents have power, the Assistant Principal had established that months ago. Some nameless, faceless parent had told the Principal that my colleague scolded her daughter. The Principal wasted no time in coming into the cafeteria and summoned us with the old fashioned teacher pointer finger gesture to "come here." The Principal gave us a stern warning and directed us to be careful how we speak. If a student is in violation, it is best to "pull their clip" which is given to the teacher at "retrieval" explaining the infraction.

Intoxicated parent standing in front of me; she has no "clip" for me to pull! What to do? Her speech was slurred. She was drunk. She moved to kindergarten table 22, dropped the McDonald's™ bag, and headed to the food counter. I decided to ask for a second opinion from a teacher coming out of the teacher's lunchroom. The teacher walked near her, looked at me, rolled her eyes and came over to say "Yeah she is wasted!" The teacher didn't know what to do either.

The drunken parent purchased a beverage and made her way to table 22 all the way at the other end of the room. Now the staff person on the register signaled holding her nose. She sat next to her daughter fussing over the little one and stroking her hair. She was enjoying the fries, her daughter and lunchtime. I told the head of the kitchen staff. Lunch ended. The teacher retrieved the class. The mother left. We were all relieved. Oh but wait....

The next week guess what? With tables settled for their lunch period, in strolls the drunken mother – still drunk along with two men in their late 30's clean and neatly dressed. No one had visitor name tags. This means they are not appropriately on school grounds or fully signed in at the office. They go directly to table 22. I walked over to ask about name tags. Before I could ask, I heard one man loud and crudely telling the little ones at the table he was buying them ice cream. Now I am there and said "Hello, good afternoon. Have you checked in at the office?" I was quickly dismissed with a slurred explanation of "....only asking to buy kids ice cream...." I recognized he was not drunk he was stoned. My colleague came over. We huddled and decided a call to the Principal was in order. The cashier and others must have seen the incident unfolding. By time the two lunch ladies got to the kitchen supervisor, the call was already made.

It was in a shake-of–a-dog's tail that the Principal entered the cafeteria. She came directly to me. By now these three have been identified as the mother, the father, and the uncle. The Principal told me they had come the other day and were somehow coming in and drove away in such a manner she almost notified the police. The Principal waited until the mother was away from the table and went to her. I had to hear, so me and my trash barrel rolled close.

The conversation was easy-breezy. There were mild soft kid glove words from the Principal. They smiled and nodded and laughed. The three inappropriate intoxicated adults had lunch and strolled out. What was different this time was others were concerned, the Principal intervened, the children at the table were unnerved and the daughter appeared embarrassed. The Principal left before the lunch period was over. She told me to keep an eye and to call her if necessary. All things considered this was better than nothing. However, I was confused. How is it, a parent can break the rules more than once and there is only chit-chat? Was there no concern for the other children? The Principal had no problem giving the lunch ladies a straight-forward firm directive "no scolding." Who is in charge here?

Seriously, who is schooling who? Drunken, stoned parents' seem to be in charge. The welfare of their daughter and her classmates' appeared to me to be abandoned. Is this the culture here of "do not rock the boat." The only position role held accountable and to a higher standard is the lowest person on the totem pole, the lunch lady(ies)!

Family

Earlier in this section, *Enter the Lunch Lady*, the parallel was made between school's cafeteria being similar to a home's kitchen and family room. It follows then that the number one topic is family in both the cafeteria and the kitchen.

Here are but a few of the family centered conversations that went on in this suburban middle class elementary school. Each is compelling, real and raw. There was a third grader who talked on a regular basis either to her grandmother in Puerto Rico or her grandmother in New York. She delighted in showing pictures and even a hand-knitted sweater from one of her grandmothers. Then, one afternoon at last lunch she told me her grandmother in Puerto Rico had died. The third grader was visibly saddened. She said "....outside I feel okay....inside I feel hurt!" She expressed a questioning of how this could be. To this day only the gentle hug was suitable in response. Her tears told me the inside and outside were becoming one. Grief is like that.

There were numerous stories of a parent going off or due to return from far off distant lands as members of the U.S. Military. It was a haunting set of questions – should a child be forced to endure? Does anyone see what the children are trying to tell adults despite their "chin-up" exterior? What are the effects on children of deployed military on their education?

Naturally, there were those moments of pure delight. First the youngster; interestingly usually first and second graders announcing they were going to get a brother or sister.

From one first grader, she was expecting twins! It was typically they who were expecting not their mother. And how much giddiness, pride and satisfaction were seen once the baby arrived. Daily reports were voluntarily, freely and frequently given. The reports slowed down as the novelty wore off, which I think correlated to sleeplessness and or lesser positioning the family.

Then there were family events that took me by surprise. One was a fifth grade girl who appeared each morning a bit dusty, tattered clothes, same worn out shoes and rather unkempt. This is not a good look for the critical and superficially competitive "tween" group. She was treated as an outcast. Each morning she'd drop her bag and quick-step to me with open arms. I suspect she was homeless. When I asked about her house the reply was muddled. I did not pursue gathering any more details as she was obviously uncomfortable talking about home or family.

The exact opposite was the case of the little guy enough with personality to fill half the room. He wanted to talk about his family all the time. I had met his mom. He seemed to ease in his life until one day he blurted out "my mom is trying to get enough money to get my dad out of Nicaragua!" Not wanting him to see my shock I took a breath and said something news, sports and weather like. He reassured me that getting his dad to the USA would happen soon.

The last surprising event in the "kitchen and family room" at school was the fifth grader who had straddled and pummeled the smaller eye-glassed classmate on the fifth day of the new school year. The first young man and I had developed nothing less than a rich meaningful relationship. So it was not unusual for him to approach me wanting to tell me something in his mind of great importance. It was a hectic moment. I wanted to give him my undivided attention (best one can in the midst of the activity).

I sweetly attempted to waive him off. It didn't work. He was persistent. He was literally grinning and bouncing, like "Tigger," "...but I gotta tell you!" My "give me one minute" was falling on deaf ears. I stopped. I turned and gave in smiling, "What is it?" (This "it better be good" was unspoken). All in one concise motion the now taller than me student placed his right arm fully around my shoulders, let go a smile undeniably brilliant and announced, "My dad is coming home from prison this Friday!"

A fifth grade boy unashamedly giving and getting a hug in full sight of a room of peers. His joy was my joy in that moment. On my drive home each word of the student's good news stood up; "My dad is coming home from prison on Friday." Then again an auto-replay "....home from prison..."

How do we get a grip on what all today and tomorrow's children have to live with in their homes? In their lives? These are only a handful; five home life events. There are countless more. And how many more do teachers come to know? In what ways does the educational system assist, support, resource or merely acknowledge the full scope of a child's life?

There was a time, many decades pass when the events that surprised were perhaps divorce or an out-of-wedlock birth in the family. Now the list is long and impacts deeply. Our children are people too. The current set-up in this learning environment must take into consideration the emotional, mental, physical, psychological and spiritual state of students. Education as is under rates the anxiety, anger and fear as well as over rating students stamina and problem-solving ability.

Yet students are complex enough that their intuition, insight and manipulative skills have to be taken into account.

Lessons Learned

Right about now you may wonder, what about the food? The food was not a priority. Students have come to understand the cafeteria is not about food. It is about coping with whatever is placed in front of you. If that doesn't work then go to the snack bar for more sugars and carbs and yippee this sugar is not disguised; it is what it is.

The alternative to school lunch is bring your own or have one of your people (mom, dad, grandparents, neighbors) deliver outside food to you. Give them your lunchtime and table number and you're "good to go!"

Meet the Wizard

The support staff, particularly "The Lunch Lady" is seeing behind the great curtain to meet The Wizard. The Wizard's lesson is, we adults including parents, teachers, guardians, community at large, politicians, lunch ladies all of us must come together. We must identify our talents and knowledge to form a combined effort to transform education.

We must trust we already have the teachings the students need and want. We must muster our will and renew our self-confidence to meet the challenge. The one challenge is how to deliver the foundational lessons. We like Dorothy, Scarecrow, Lion, Tin Man and the Oz gang must admit we only think we are deficient which causes a sense of being lost. There is not lost-ness when we successfully adapt to the land we are in.

Everyone has to be at the table in mapping out education's critically needed revisions. Staff meetings in schools need to include faculty, administrators, family and support staff representation because each role contributes to the whole of a student's education.

Support Staff

One comes to recognize being "The Lunch Lady," custodian, bus driver, office worker means your status is tenuous at best. It is best to go about your assigned task humbly; while exerting the wisdom of "The Dog Whisperer." It is a thin, fine line walked every day. One day you are a rock star the next a doormat. Does this sound familiar? Something akin to being a parent! But here is the central lesson; keep perspective and be careful to check your ego in the parking lot.

Next Generation

You may think this is about the 21st Century child. It is and it isn't. Keeping pace with what youngsters know and their inner Sanctum is impossible.

They come into the world already prepared for living in a different time than adults. Our work is to give them necessary tools to find their own way in making positive contributions to all society.

Perhaps the "Prime Directive" from Gene Roddenberry's Star Trek begins to readjust our challenge. The directive is there *can be no interference with the internal development of other beings*. **Interpreting that for our role with youngsters may suggest our allowing more opportunities for the 21st Century beings to show us the way.**

In the Immediate

What would it take if right now the educational system declared:

1. Every public school needs to have a staffing that reflects its student population.

    Students are watching adults all the time. Human nature continues to be 'do as seen not as said'. Every student deserves and desires seeing themselves in all possible roles. Tell me a story of an art teacher and let me see myself in the story.

2. Every public school needs to create quality supervised time during the school day. This means lunch time is for a meal. Time enough to sit, catch your breath and chew your food! Guided Socialization? Preparatory and parochial school models may be helpful. Having an adult, parent, teacher, staffer at the table to guide conversation and to support the practice of table manners.

3. Along with a more civilized mealtime, teachers too deserve and desire a moment to refresh and refuel. The more renewed the teacher, the better the lesson.

4. Adequate support staffing for safety sake. A bus full of children needs more than one adult. School buses need at least one adult to oversee students and one to drive.

5. A systematic exchange amongst support staff, teachers, administration and parents/guardians. The model suggested here is a monthly "roundtable" concerning each class. This would be an authentic team approach.

One Among Millions or a Million to One?

by Mark Stallworth

The implication from the question is this: Dorothy is an average youngster, but is her experience likely or not likely to happen again?

Dorothy is not better or worse than any other child. In the *Wizard of Oz* story, Dorothy is having a uniquely unusual experience. It would appear she saw herself as fortunate even in the midst of a life changing challenge. She was one surely of many others trying their utmost to find their place - their 'way home.' Dorothy and her story is representative. Dorothy is a representative example, and be clear there are countless other *Dorothy's* with their very own unique story. Dorothy is due respect, applause and admiration for every bit of her outstanding accomplishment.

If Dorothy did it so can others…if and when given the necessary support. What follows is a contemporary youngster's story. It is one we can identify with because it once was familiar; even common. It once was "one among millions." Again, no better no worse than countless others; the haunting question is "will there be others if we do not repair the educational system?" Our current and future youngsters desperately need support in finding their way home.

Learning About Learning, Teaches us About Teaching

Not unlike Dorothy, my story is a representation of being a product of education. My "yellow-brick road" began in Ann Arbor, Michigan. There are portions of my journey that had to be told to me as I was too young to remember. There was, in those days, no such thing as Pre-K; however, there was Head Start. I can only recall the yellow school bus that faithfully picked me up right from my home. It was exciting! We called it, "the squished-up" bus because it was not a regular full-sized school bus. Every morning appeared my teacher with an ear-to-ear smile to hold my hand as we boarded to greet the bus-driver. Even though it was only a half day, I thought of myself as a "big boy."

I graduated from Head Start and moved on to elementary school. Three main things stand out in my early memories of learning. The first memory is the positive affect and the pleasant balance of diversity our classes and school had. I recall riding the big bus through the neighborhood of The University of Michigan's Married Student Housing, Northwood V, where I lived with my Mother and Father. I heard the grown-ups call the housing, "a little U.N."(United Nations). The second notable recollection about school was the social interaction 1st and 2nd grades were far more fun, exciting and important than the daily lessons of practicing penmanship or arithmetic. And then there is the third memory of the school that I so enjoyed attending. It is a memory which has left a blemish with me as a person. The blemish came about due to the then accepted memorization method of teaching reading. It wasn't until 4th grade when we moved to Rochester, New York that the method of phonetics came up on my educational path.

While this teaching difference seemed miniscule to many, and was likely brushed off as a regional educational difference, it was the wound of my educational flesh whose scar would not fade easily or quickly. Entering a new school for a child is difficult enough. I felt different beyond being the "new kid." How easily a change in teaching methods can be turned into a perceived learning impediment. It was my mom who held me steady and helped me maintain my confidence and dignity. It was also my mom who figured out what the learning obstacle was.

She was a working single-parent and yet made me her number one priority always. She was constantly at school talking with my teacher and the principal. She was the "middle person" between my new school in Rochester, New York and my former school in Ann Arbor, Michigan. Yet this bump on my "yellow-brick road" did not stop me from learning to read, making friends, and years later graduating from The University of Michigan, Ann Arbor; as did my mother and father before me. This is all to amplify the importance of parental involvement and a school's need to discern prior methods of teaching basics. What one may consider insignificant and only slightly relevant, one's teaching method during a child's crucial developmental year's shapes, molds, and impacts how a child feels about him/herself.

While Dorothy met "Scarecrow" and other characters I met "hoops" (basketball). Hoops became my life's third rail. It was the spark that kept me moving forward. I lived basketball. More importantly, basketball was the center of my educational career. I'm sure this was (and is) the same for many other pre-teen kids. I was a young teenage boy bouncing my basketball around the streets of Northwest Detroit with hoop dreams that included a shiny mustang convertible. In a strange way, basketball was the bridge between maintaining social acceptance outside of the class room and academic eligibility within the classroom. Ask any school's student/ athletes from elementary to high school, and they will tell you, "They won't let you play on the team without a passing GPA." Well, I was one of those student- athletes that didn't have to be told twice in this regard. Even in the 7th grade, I was so focused on being eligible to play on the middle school varsity hoops team, I accidentally made the honor roll. Suddenly, maybe more so by myself, I experienced being looked at differently by classmates, teachers, and principals, as well as family and friends. I was respected in a different light. And that light was good!

Living in dormitories for four years starting from the 9th grade added to my wonderful summers at basketball (and computer) camps which made my education pleasantly rounded. I can honestly say these are the places where a person truly learns the difference between being educated and getting "schooled."

Very importantly, I learned I had the capability and was equipped academically to satisfy the grade point average requirements which some of my counterparts did not. I did witness some of the best players fall short academically. Academic failings, of course, were sometimes overlooked by the school for the sake of the boosters or the team having good chances at championships. Where does the educational system place its importance? Is it in stressing to the student- athlete their academics first or their sport?

To be sure as an adult, I've come to recognize what as a child I did not see or understand; family, friends and community played such a significant role in helping me "find my place." Family sets the tone and example.

I do not know a time any option other than college and family were ever placed in front of me. College was a given. My say was which college and what degree. Friends and community knowingly entered into the college conspiracy...for which I am grateful.

Position Change

One's position changes as one's position changes. My position change includes looking at our educational system from the vantage point of a practicing attorney; as well as a husband and father.
For the sake of this contribution let me start with the law.

1954 The U.S. Supreme Court gave this opinion to become the 'law of the land': "Today, education is perhaps the most important function of state and local governments."

> *Compulsory school attendance laws and the great expenditures for education both demonstrate our recognition of the importance of education to our democratic society. It is required in the performance of our most basic public responsibilities, even service in the armed forces. It is the very foundation of good citizenship. Today it is a principal instrument in awakening the child to cultural values, in preparing him for later professional training, and in helping him to adjust normally to his environment. In these days, it is doubtful that any child may reasonably be expected to succeed in life if he is denied the opportunity of an education. Such an opportunity, where the state has undertaken to provide it, is a right which must be made available to all on equal terms."*

-Brown v. Board of Education 347 U.S. 483 (1954) (USSC+) (30)

From that day on, there was to be a change of social attitude that was to shift, in a sense, the undercurrent of our capitalistic society that made it go from 'its ok to work and school is a luxury,' to 'education is a necessity to survive and it's a right!' All these years, decades later we are witnessing the sad let down of education in America. What we are seeing today seems to be the commercialization, businessized, "happy meal'ing®" of education; which reflects in the underlying disconnect between our society's seemingly agreed on recognition of the importance of education, and at the same time a lack of respect for the craft of teaching as a science and profession.

From the onslaught of online colleges to the chain-care daycare franchises; across the board we are realizing there is a dichotomy. On one hand teachers are accepted as the second most important beings in our children's everyday life and rearing. And yet, teachers are paid the least and are, more often than not, demanded upon the most. On a daily basis teachers have to deal with serious behavioral issues, lack of involvement from home, under-funding and struggles with administrators. What other profession has such a constant "uphill" battle? We wonder why quality teachers are leaving and the attraction to others is virtually non-existent? It is imperative as a nation we take on the task to attract and retain the brightest and best talents into a new school system.

I am one among millions grateful to and for the teachers we had along our "yellow-brick road." Our stories are made unique because they are highly personal. The importance of each of the millions of stories is to raise the timely and critical questions. Will there be countless millions to follow? Will there be millions more to complete their journey well, making positive contributions to America's, and the world's society? Or, are we in America's educational history creating the odds of only "a million to one" who will succeed? The odds will depend on our banding together immediately and with urgency to change the current U.S. education system. For me and millions of others we count ourselves fortunate. I can reflect on my educational experience; ranging from public school, to parochial school, to private exemplary boarding school with tears of pride and smiles of gratitude. As I once heard another one among million say, "Looking back, my most important outfit and fashion statement was a cap and gown."

"If we as a Nation keep pulling left and right we will never move forward."
Cory Booker, Mayor, Newark, New Jersey.

The Proposal "Lift Every Voice..."
by Lynnette Stallworth

The yellow brick road led somewhere and the Wizard had something to say. All the efforts by the characters had a pay-off. We end our journey through **Who's Schooling Who?** with a proposal.

It is proposed the Secretary of Education convene The National Conference to Transform Education in America*.

The Secretary of Education will be responsible for bringing participants together and outlining an agenda in such a way to produce a step-by-step recommendation (road-map/plan) for real change including a timeline and funding options.

The Secretary of Education will be responsible for assembling a pre-conference team to plan, design and outline the conference. The team would need to be dedicated to strong outcomes; including but not limited to "An American Pledge to Education." It may be appropriate to have the conference participants formulate particular group oaths (administrators, teachers, parents, guardians, etc.) much like being sworn into a committed organization.

*This is not a "meeting." This is not just a "conversation." This is not a "gathering." *THIS IS AN ACTION TAKING GROUP* to bring remedy to the education system. The conference is to "get it done," "right the ship," "just do it," "get off the pot," "now is the time;

the time is now," "be the change."*

<u>Invited</u> as participants are those reflective of the demographic make-up of the country.

- The following needs to be a cross-section by regions (North, South, Middle, East and West).

    - Inner city, rural, urban and suburban.

    - Lower, middle, upper-middle, upper wealthy and poor.

    - Top, middle, lower tiered educators (not struggling to destitute).

- There must be a proportional number of persons according to America's diversity.

There is a place and task for everyone in this united effort.

- Hearing from grassroots, frontline persons is primary to the conference.

- Those that have not had access and headlines will be given preference. Media would be asked to support this significant task by maintaining a position outside the confines of the conference. Like "no smoking" zones, the conference will have "no media" areas. Perhaps the working model could be similar to that of C-Span's coverage of Congress. The media will be asked and expected to report checked facts only; not opinions and/or conjecture. "Talking heads" would be discouraged. Media would be asked to set a goal and maintain a coverage standard of being informative (factual) verses entertaining (trivial).

- The Conference should use the very best facilities to lead the assemblies. The facilitators may also be asked to make input to designing the process with purpose as the ultimate focus.

The design for process will do well to have an understanding of participant's behavior. Participants will be expected to behave as exemplary adult role models. Inability to behave to Conference standards may cause permanent dismissal (as a participant.)

- The Conference will benefit having students and teachers as center circle to the issues, next circle parents/guardians with administrators in the next circle and all others part of surrounding circle. The two groups on the "front line" are the students and teachers. They know what they know about day-to-day dynamics at school. They need the active support of all others.

Lift Every Voice Model

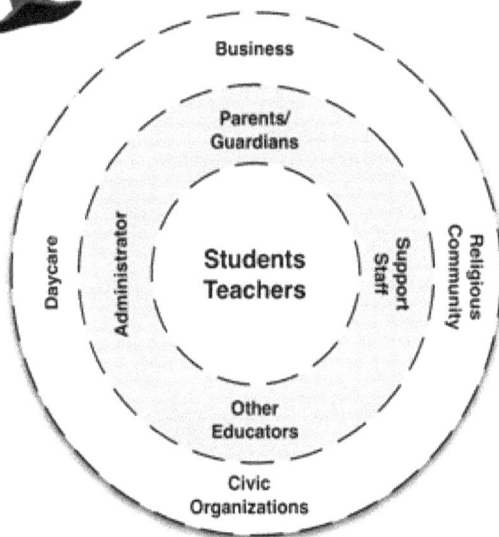

Government has the responsibility of fully funding education. School boards and administrators are obligated to make sure resources get to where they are needed when they are needed.

We, the people have the duty to hold local, state, federal government, boards, principals, teachers, other parents and guardians and students consistently accountable for the measurable success of America's public school system. No need to blame because we all bare some shame. (31)

In this eleventh hour there must be a banding together, being united for the good of our nation.

Our children are watching us…

The time is now…now is the time for a framework of *forward motion*.

Will education be a "too late" issue as gas/fuel/oil and other issues have become? There will be no Organization of Petroleum Exporting Countries (OPEC) or oil companies to blame. Not resolving education with immediate urgent and dedicated transformation of education in America will be no one's fault but our own. Are you ready to live with the consequences of no action?

Lift Every Voice & Sing often called the Negro National Anthem is a song written as a poem by James Weldon Johnson (1871 - 1938) and set to music by his brother John Rosamond Johnson (1873-1954) in 1900.

What Will You Do?
Who's Schooling Who? Conclusion
by Veronica Brown

Who's Schooling Who? is a call for action and advocacy. This book project provides a kaleidoscope of experiences, ideas and perspectives on the current American public education system. Every writer sets a scene, describes the major characters and hints at a slight glimmer of hope for needed changes and transformation in today's educational system. The book contributors report and describe personal experiences that motivate them to actively involve themselves in altering the current educational system in this country. Very convincing arguments are presented for instructing students in moral, character and spiritual building, as well as proven scholastic and academic programs which augment students' natural talent. *Who's Schooling Who?* has shown "wizard-like" information, insight and instruction concerning matters of economics in relation to education. Every contributor alludes to the national and local struggles surrounding inadequate funding, management and accountability. How and why are our children not learning what we know they should? What are our students telling us about the nature and purpose of today's schooling?

As the political and spiritual leader, Mahatma Gandhi emphatically asserted, "We must become the change we want to see." Each reader of this book has to commit to becoming a change agent. When Dorothy and her three friends in the world renown fairy tale, *The Wizard of Oz* went in search of the wizard to fulfill their demands, he was wise and clever enough to recognize they had the power to grant their own wishes. Dorothy wanted to return home, a place of comfort and familiarity, and her friends wanted a brain, heart and courage. Ironically, American school children want the same attributes; they tell us in what we perceive, depending on our perspective and position, in positive and negative ways. This book is not a call for transformation, the transformation has already occurred. If we watch, listen and talk with our students as they travel the yellow brick road hoping to find a wizard, we will not be puzzled and frustrated when determining what course of action to take.

First, we have to rotate the lens of our various kaleidoscopes and become

comfortable with the process of learning a multi-perspective approach to managing the educational changes and results shared by the writers in this book. Unlike Dorothy, we should not want to return to the place we consider comfortable and even effective. Today's schools should not look, act or respond to societal trends the way they did 20 or 10 years ago. Our students tell and show us a spirit that wants to imagine, create and do. Schools today reflect societal changes and in an effort to manage the changes, courses of study such as art, geography and physical education are limited, or eliminated. We who see must become a cog in the wheel, work to revive the spirit of education in one classroom, one school, one district... Act and advocate. Focused action coupled with persistent advocacy can renew our schools and our children's hearts.

Second, we must lead by example. Do we model courage for our children? Are we hesitant to question because we focus our intellectual and spiritual lens on those presented as authority figures? Written requests for information, noncombative questions, casual school visits, monitoring of school board meeting notes and policies, disseminating proposed educational recommendations and appointments are a few pertinent methods for advocating and ensuring the needs of our children are not only addressed, but also met. One letter and/or email sent to the correct agency and policymaker can create a cascade of corrective actions. For example; when was the last time the questions concerning guidance and counseling programs have been raised? As our children speak about and react to the stresses of today's school accountability management style, we must embrace the courage to respond: advocate, refute and reward.

Lastly, we can use our intellect, brains to build capacity, and broaden our spheres of influence. The family unit, which can be challenging, is the most logical and advantageous group to begin practicing advocacy and action with. Social, religious, political and community organizations can also provide avenues for developing strategic, effective approaches to successfully manage educational change. Many believe if we have no children attending educational institutions, then we should not be actively involved in determining education policies.

As a society, and culture, we cannot chance letting someone or something become the change we want to see. If while reading this book, you experienced some frustration, began to wonder why, and recognized several scenes and characters, then you have the stamina to act and advocate. Our children are watching and waiting; they expect us to guide them in how to become the change we want to see.

What will you do? - WWYD

A Brief History of Education: A Timeline(32)

1635 - The first Latin Grammar School (Boston Latin School) is established. Latin Grammar Schools are designed for sons of certain social classes who are destined for leadership positions in church, state, or the courts. The first "free school" in Virginia opens. However, education in the Southern colonies is more typically provided at home by parents or tutors.

1636 - Harvard College, the first higher education institution in what is now the United States, is established in Newtowne (now Cambridge), Massachusetts.

1693 - The College of William and Mary is established in Virginia.

1698 - The first publicly supported library in the U.S. is established in Charles Town, South Carolina. Two years later, the General Assembly of South Carolina passes the first public library law.

1751 - Benjamin Franklin helps to establish the first "English Academy" in Philadelphia with a curriculum that is both classical and modern, including such courses as history, geography, navigation, surveying, and modern as well as classical languages. The academy ultimately becomes the University of Pennsylvania.

1779 – Thomas Jefferson proposes a two-track educational system, with different tracks for "the laboring and the learned."

1787 - The Young Ladies Academy opens in Philadelphia and becomes the first academy for girls in America.

1821 - The first public high school, Boston English High School, opens .

1837 - Eighty students arrive at Mount Holyoke Female Seminary, the first college for women in the U.S. Its founder/president is Mary Lyon. The African Institute (later called the Institute for Colored Youth) opens in Cheyney, Pennsylvania. Now called Cheyney University, is the oldest institution of higher learning for African Americans.

1853 - Pennsylvania begins funding the Pennsylvania Training School for Feeble-Minded Children, a private school for children with intellectual disabilities.

1867 - The Department of Education is created in order to help states establish effective school systems.

1879 - The first Native American boarding school opens in Carlisle, Pennsylvania. It becomes the model for a total of 26 similar schools, all with the goal of assimilating Native American children into the mainstream culture.

1890 - The Second Morrill Act is enacted. It provides for the "more complete endowment and support of the colleges" through the sale of public lands. Part of this funding leads to the creation of 16 historically black land-grant colleges.

1892 - The Committee on Secondary Social Studies, often called the Committee of Ten, recommends a college-oriented high school curriculum.

1900 - The Association of American Universities is founded to promote higher standards and put U.S. universities on an equal footing with their European counterparts.

1904 - Mary McLeod Bethune, an African American educator, founds the Daytona Educational and Industrial Training School for Negro Girls in Daytona Beach, Florida. It merges with the Cookman Institute in 1923 and becomes a coeducational high school, which eventually evolves into Bethune-Cookman College, now Bethune-Cookman University.

1913 - Edward Lee Thorndike's book, *Educational Psychology: The Psychology of Learning*, is published. It describes his theory that human learning involves habit formation, or connections between stimuli (or situations as Thorndike preferred to call them) and responses (Connectionism). He believes that such connections are strengthened by repetition ("Law of Exercise") and achieving satisfying consequences ("Law of Effect"). These ideas, which contradict traditional faculty psychology and mental discipline, come to dominate American educational psychology for much of the Twentieth Century and greatly influence American educational practice.

1916 - The Bureau of Educational Experiments is founded in New York City by Lucy Sprague Mitchell with the purpose of studying child development and children's learning.

1917 - The Smith-Hughes Act passes, providing federal funding for agricultural and vocational education.

1919 - The Progressive Education Association is founded with the goal of reforming American education. All states have laws providing funds for transporting children to school.

1922 - Abigail Adams Eliot, with help from Mrs. Henry Greenleaf Pearson, establishes the Ruggles Street Nursery School in Roxbury, MA, one of the first educational nursery schools in the U.S.

1939 - The Wechsler Adult Intelligence Scale (first called the Wechsler-Bellevue Intelligence Scale) is developed by David Wechsler. It introduces the concept of the "deviation IQ," which calculates IQ scores based on how far subjects' scores differ (or deviate) from the average (mean) score of others who are the same age, rather than calculating them with the ratio (MA/CA multiplied by 100) system. Wechsler intelligence tests, particularly the Wechsler Intelligence Scale for Children, are still widely used in U.S. schools to help identify students needing special education.

1963 - Samuel A. Kirk uses the term "learning disability" at a Chicago conference on children with perceptual disorders.

1965 - The Elementary and Secondary Education Act (ESEA) is passed on April 9. Part of Lyndon Johnson's "War on Poverty," it provides federal funds to help low-income students, which results in the initiation of educational programs such as Title I and bilingual education. Project Head Start, a preschool education program for children from low-income families, begins as an eight-week summer program. Part of the "War on Poverty," the program continues to this day as the longest-running anti-poverty program in the U.S.

1968 - The Bilingual Education Act, also known as Title VII, becomes law. After many years of controversy, the law is repealed in 2002 and replaced by the No Child Left Behind Act. McCarver Elementary School in Tacoma, Washington becomes the nation's first magnet school.

1969 - Herbert R. Kohl's book, *The Open Classroom*, helps to promote open education, an approach emphasizing student-centered classrooms and active, holistic learning. The conservative back-to-the-basics movement of the 1970s begins at least partially as a backlash against open education.

1970 - Jean Piaget's book, *The Science of Education,* is published. His Learning Cycle model helps to popularize discovery-based teaching approaches, particularly in the sciences. The case of Diana v. California State Board results in new laws requiring that children referred for possible special education placement be tested in their primary language.

1971 - In the case of Pennsylvania Association for Retarded Children (PARC) v. Pennsylvania, the federal court rules that students with mental retardation are entitled to a free public education.

1972 - Title IX of the Education Amendments of 1972 becomes law. Though many people associate this law only with girl's and women's participation in sports, Title IX prohibits discrimination based on sex in all aspects of education. The Marland Report to Congress on gifted and talented education is issued. It recommends a broader definition of giftedness that is still widely accepted today.

1973 - The Rehabilitation Act becomes law. Section 504 of this act guarantees civil rights for people with disabilities in the context of federally funded institutions and requires accommodations in schools including participation in programs and activities as well as access to buildings. Today, "504 Plans" are used to provide accommodations for students with disabilities who do not qualify for special education or an IEP.

1981 - John Holt's book, *Teach Your Own: A Hopeful Path for Education,* adds momentum to the homeschooling movement.

1982 - In the case of Board of Education v. Pico , the U.S. Supreme court rules that books cannot be removed from a school library because school administrators deemed their content to be offensive.

1984 - Public Law 105-332, the Carl D. Perkins Vocational and Technical Education Act, is passed with the goal of increasing the quality of vocational-technical education in the U.S. It is reauthorized in 1998 and again in 2006 as the Carl D. Perkins Vocational and Technical Education

Act (PL 109-270). The Emergency Immigrant Education Act is enacted to provide services and offset the costs for school districts that have unexpectedly large numbers of immigrant students.

1994 - The Improving America's Schools Act (IASA) is signed into law by President Bill Clinton on January 25th. It. reauthorizes the ESEA of 1965 and includes reforms for Title I; increased funding for bilingual and immigrant education; and provisions for public charter schools, drop-out prevention, and educational technology. CompHigh is founded. It claims to be the first online high school.

1998 - California voters pass Proposition 227, requiring that all public school instruction be in English. This time the law withstands legal challenges. The Higher Education Act is amended and reauthorized requiring institutions and states to produce "report cards" about teacher education (See Title II).

1999- K12 launches as an online educational tool developed to provide any child access to exceptional curriculum and tools that enable him or her to maximize his or her success in life, regardless of geographic, financial, or demographic circumstance.

2001 - The controversial No Child Left Behind Act (NCLB) is approved by Congress and signed into law by President George W. Bush on January 8, 2002. The law, which reauthorizes the ESEA of 1965 and replaces the Bilingual Education Act of 1968, mandates high-stakes student testing, holds schools accountable for student achievement levels, and provides penalties for schools that do not make adequate yearly progress toward meeting the goals of NCLB.

2003 - The North American Council for Online Learning (NACOL), a non-profit organization dedicated to enhancing K-12 online education, is "launched as a formal corporate entity."

2004 - H.R. 1350, The Individuals with Disabilities Improvement Act (IDEA 2004), reauthorizes and modifies IDEA. Changes, which take effect on **July 1, 2005** included modifications in the IEP process and procedural safeguards, increased authority for school personnel in special education placement decisions, and alignment of IDEA with the No Child Left

Behind Act of 2001.

2009 - The American Reinvestment and Recovery Act of 2009 provides more than 90-billion dollars for education, nearly half of which goes to local school districts to prevent layoffs and for school modernization and repair. It includes the Race to the Top initiative, a 4.35-billion-dollar program designed to induce reform in K-12 education. For more information on the impact of the Recovery Act on education, go to ED.gov. Quest to Learn (Q2L), the first school to teach primarily through game-based learning, opens in September in New York City with a class of sixth graders There are plans to add a grade each year until the school serves students in grades six through twelve.

References

1) Gladwell, Malcolm (2008, November). *Outliers: The Story of Success.* Little, Brown & Company.

2) Florida Sunshine State Standards (1996). http://www.fldoe.org/bii/curriculum/sss/sss1996.asp

3) Frey, N. (2005). *Retention, Social Promotion, and Academic Redshirting: What Do We Know and Need to Know? Remedial & Special Education*, 26(6), 332-346.

4) Jimerson, S., & Kaufman, A. (2003, April). *Reading, Writing, and Retention: A primer on Grade Retention Research. Reading Teacher*, 56(7), 622.

5) Teaching Tolerance. Southern Poverty Law Center. http://www.splcenter.org/what-we-do/teaching-tolerance.

6) Walters, Andy (2009). *My Spirituality as an Atheist.* www.YouTube.com.

7) Friedman, Cary A. (2007). *Spiritual Survival for Law Enforcement.* Compass Press.

8) Williamson, Marianne (1992). *A Return to Love.* Harper Collins.

9) Boynton, Sandra (1982). *Moo, Baa, La La La.* Simon & Schuster.

10) http://www.all4ed.org/publication_material/understanding_HSgradrates.

11) Bowler, M. (2009, August, 19). U.S. News and World Report. *Drop Outs Loom Large for Schools.* http://www.usnews.com/

education/best-colleges/articles/2009/08/19/dropouts-loom-large-for-schools.html

12) Lewis, S., Simon, C., Uzzell, R, Horwitz, A, Casserly, M. (2010, October). *A Call for Change, The Social and Educational Factors Contributing to the Outcomes of Black Males in Urban Schools.*

13) Bennett, J.L. (2009, March 29). *Many college students face a mountain of debt once they graduate.* www.Democratand Chronicle.com http://www.democratandchronicle.com/article/20090329/NEWS01/903290339/Many-college-students-face-mountain-of-debt-once-they-graduate.

14) CNN (2008, December, 5). http://money.cnn.com/2008/12/05/news/economy/degreed_workers/index.htm.

15) Huffington Post. www.huffingtonpost.com.

16) CNN. www.cnn.com.

17) Hillsborough County Public Schools. (2010, April, 5). *Financial Handbook Budget.*

18) The Florida Department of Education (2010). http://fldoe.org/fefp/pdf/fefpdist.pdf. Pages 11-12.

19) The Florida State Lottery (2010). *Dollars to Education.* www.floridalottery.com.

20) The Missouri State Lottery (2010). *Where the Money Goes.* www.molottery.com.

21) *The Common School Journal.* Horace Mann.

22) Kozol, Jonathan (1991). *Savage Inequalities.* New York: Crown Publishers.

23) *Trends in Educational Funding—Public Schools: Where Does the Money Come From?* http://social.jank.org/page973/.

24) U.S. Department of Education (2010). *A Blueprint for Reform.* Washington, DC.

25) Cohen, Ashley (1996). *The Power of Team.* http://inside.nike.com/ blogs/nikewomen-en_US/2009/04/27/the-power-of-team.

26) Wikipedia. www.wikipedia.com.

27) *Stages of Adolescence.* www.babyart.org.

28) The Huffington Post (2011, July, 26). *Meth Teacher? Little Kid Makes Hilarious Misspelling.* www.HuffingtonPost.com.

29) Wiseman, Rosalind, Rapoport, Elizabeth (2006). *Queen Bee Moms and Kingpin Dads: Dealing with the Difficult Parents in Your Child's Life.* Crown Publishing.

30) Brown v Board of Education (1954). United States Supreme Court.

31) Johnson, James Weldon (1871-1938), Johnson, John Rosamond *Lift Every Voice* (1873- 1954).

32) American Educational History: A Hypertext Timeline http://www. cloudnet.com/~edrbsass/educationhistorytimeline.html.

BIOGRAPHIES
Contributing Authors

Veronica E. Brown

Veronica was born in Baltimore, Maryland. She grew up in Mount Vernon, New York and has lived in Boston, Massachusetts, Washington, DC, Monmouth County, New Jersey, Saint Louis, Missouri, Detroit, Michigan, and Orlando, Florida.

Veronica has earned degrees from Hampton University (BS), Hampton, Virginia, The American University (MA), Washington, D.C. and Notre Dame University (M.ED), Baltimore, Maryland.

Her teaching experience spans middle school, high school, and on the college level. She has also worked as a Principal, Superintendent Designee, and Chief Academic Officer.

Along with other professional achievements, Veronica has been a presenter at numerous national, state and local conferences. Veronica is published in The English Journal, Fairfax Writing Teachers Journal, and The Teacher As Researcher.

In her leisure, "Roni" enjoys family time and traveling.

April Griffin

April Griffin was first elected to the Hillsborough County School Board in 2006 and she was re-elected in 2010. She is one of seven members responsible for making policy decisions and overseeing a budget of $3.1 billion for the 8th largest school district in the nation.

April has been a member of the PTA, a classroom volunteer and active in her children's schools for many years. Prior to her full-time commitment to the school board, she was a successful business owner and long time child and elder advocate. April has championed changing the policy of "retired and rehired at same pay level."

She currently serves on the national board of directors of Youth Crime Watch of America, the Juvenile Justice Board, the Hillsborough County Council of Governments, and the Hillsborough Kids Healthcare Foundation. She is a Tampa Chamber of Commerce Leadership Tampa alumna. April promotes vocational education and says, "…college is an admirable goal, but it is not everyone's reality."

April was born, reared, and educated in Hillsborough County. She has been married to Brian Griffin for 19 years and they are the proud parents of two sons who attend Hillsborough County public schools.

John C. Harvey

A native of Detroit, Michigan, John comes from a family of educators. His education includes A Bachelors of Arts from Wabash College and a Master's of Divinity from Yale Divinity School. He is a Fellow in Pastoral Leadership Development, Princeton Theological Seminary.

John has been an Instructor of Philosophy; as well as Director of United Campus Christian Ministry at Wayne State University in the cultural-heart of Detroit, Michigan.

John has lived in Crawfordsville, Indiana, Philadelphia, Pennsylvania and New Haven, Connecticut.

He is an avid traveler; treasuring time with his family and friends.

Deirdra Paulk

Dierdra is an educator of many years. She graduated from Florida State University with a Bachelor and Masters degree in Exceptional Student Education.

Dierdra was born in Miami, Florida and she is now a resident of Tampa, Florida where she lives with her husband and three children.

Mark Stallworth

Mark is a partner in the law firm of Smith and Stallworth, P.A. in Tampa, Florida where he is a practicing plaintiff's attorney. Prior to private practice, Mark was an Assistant Prosecutor for the Florida. Mark earned his Juris Doctorate (J.D.) from Stetson University College of Law, Gulfport, Florida.

Mark is the product of public, parochial and private school education and he was born in Ann Arbor, Michigan. As a youngster, he lived in Rochester in Upstate New York then he returned to Michigan and graduated from Cranbrook Schools (Bloomfield).

Before graduating from The University of Michigan (Ann Arbor), he pledged Alpha Phi Alpha Fraternity, Epsilon Chapter. Mark is also a member of the Fraternal Order of Masons, Golden Square Number 35. Mark is an active contributor in the Tampa Bay community and he is a sports enthusiast.

Mark delights in family time with his wife, Selena and their son.

Interviewees

Denise Lindsay-Blue

Dr. Lindsay-Blue is an accredited (American Psychological Association) Child Clinical Psychologist and a Licensed Mental Health Counselor. Her PhD is from Alliant International University, California School of Professional Psychology.

Dr. Lindsay-Blue has taught Psychology as an Adjunct Professor (St. Petersburg College) and Middle School Special Education (grades 6, 7, 8, 9).

She has lived in New York City, Los Angeles, California and St. Petersburg, Florida.

Irene B. Johnston

Irene has been an educator for 35 years during which time she has taught elementary school including Kindergarten, 2nd and 3rd grades.

Irene is a graduate of the University of Tampa where she earned a Bachelors degree in Elementary Education with a minor in Early Childhood Development.

Irene was born in New York City; however, she has lived primarily in the Tampa Bay area of Florida most of her adult life.

Irene and her husband, Floyd, take pleasure as movie goers. Irene while not a botanist is a lover of flowers and gardening.

Lawrence Johnson, Jr.

Lawrence "Law" Johnson, Jr. has vast experience in law enforcement some of which includes: Criminal Law, Interviews and Interrogations, Crime Scene, Police Laser Operator Instructor, Police Solo Motorcycle Course, Investigative Interview, Narcotics Identification and Investigation, Close Quarter Countermeasures, Field Training Officer, and Cybersex Safety.

"Law" attended Manor College, Jacksonville Theological Seminary and Northeast Florida Criminal Justice Training Center, Institute of Police Technology & Management. He holds a B.A. in Business Administration and M.A. in Biblical Studies and Christian Psychology.

Having been School Resource Officer and currently Head Football Coach, "Law" was named NIKE® Clinics Coach of the Year by Florida Athletic Coaches Associations.

Mr. Johnson's birthplace is Jacksonville, Florida. He has also lived in Hawaii and Pennsylvania.

Danon D. Ferguson

Danon is a graduate of The University of Michigan (Ann Arbor) and Wayne State University (Detroit). His Bachelor of Science degree is in Education (Major- Physics, Minor- Mathematics). Danon's Master's of Business Administration is in Finance and Business Management. He has earned accreditation from the States of Michigan and Georgia with Certifications in Physics (6th -12th grade) and Math (6th -12th grade).

Danon has been a public school mathematics teacher for more than a decade and his teaching career is dedicated to inner-city settings. Danon is a member in good standing of Alpha Phi Alpha, Beta Gamma Sigma and Golden Key International Honor Society.

While Danon's place of birth is Detroit, Michigan, he, his wife and two children are transplants in Atlanta, Georgia.

Editors

Ushanda Pauling

Ushanda is a graduate of Springfield College, in Tampa, Florida with a Master's of Science in Mental Health Counseling. She is a Nationally Certified Youth Development Trainer through the National Training Institute, Washington D.C.

Ushanda began her professional career with the Tampa Metro Area YMCA as a Youth Program Director. She is the founder of, Leading Youth, A Universal Partnership, Inc., (L.A.Y U.P.), which is a training and consulting company created to assist agencies, organizations, and individuals with program and curriculum development. In addition, L.A.Y U.P. offers hands on training to demonstrate how to successfully operate youth development programs.

Ushanda has designed and implement additional programs such as: Start Talking!© - a group icebreaker, Gurlz on the Go™ - an adolescent girls wellness program.

Ushanda was born in Syracuse New York and at a young age, she and her family relocated to Florida. Ushanda is a former NCAA Division II collegiate women's basketball player with the University of Tampa's Lady Spartans, and majored in Exercise Science.

Ushanda's personal interests include traveling, suspense movies, being a volunteer strength and conditioning coach for high school basketball players, and amateur photography.

Veronica Blakely

Veronica Blakely is a native of Tampa, Florida where she is a Community College Instructor teaching Public Speaking, Business, and General Education courses. She is also a former high school teacher who taught Reading at an inner city school. Veronica previously worked as a manager in corporate America; however, she considers being a teacher the most important, challenging and rewarding opportunity of her career. The idea of transforming a person's mind from, "I can't" to "I can," is a humbling and rewarding experience.

Veronica is a former President and Area Governor in a Toastmaster's International Public Speaking club and she is a member of The National Speakers Association. In addition, she is a member of Delta Sigma Theta Sorority, Inc. Veronica facilitates workshops as a Communication Skills Trainer, Reading Tutor, and Life Skills Coach to inner-city youth and adults.

Veronica has a Bachelor's Degree in Speech Communication, a Master's Degree in Management, an Education Specialist Degree, and she is working on her Doctorate in Education.

Lynnette Stallworth *Editor-in-Chief*

Lynnette has lived in several parts of the United States after leaving her native home Everett in the Commonwealth of Massachusetts. Prior to retiring as an active ordained Clergywoman in the United Methodist Church, she served as the Director of the Wesley Foundation at Wayne State University (Detroit, Michigan).

A program she is particularly proud to have co-created and facilitated is "Difficult Conversations" bringing together Women of Color and Caucasian Women to dialogue on the issue of race relations.

Lynnette received her Masters of Divinity from Colgate Rochester Divinity Schools (Rochester, New York). While in seminary she was chosen the Benjamin E. Mays Scholar for two consecutive years. Her undergraduate work was done at The University of Michigan (Ann Arbor, Michigan) Maize and Blue continues to run through her veins… "Go Blue!"

As a trained transformative mediator, Lynnette has been on the roster of The United States Postal Service; as well as hearing cases for Fortune 500 Companies. Lynnette is a former Florida State Supreme Court Certified Mediator.

Lynnette enjoys the many pleasures of living in Tampa, Florida. Her greatest joy is being nearby her family.

One Hundred Years from Now

(excerpt from "Within My Power" by Forest Witcraft)

One Hundred Years from now
It will not matter
What kind of car I drove,
What kind of house I lived in,
How much money was in my bank account
Nor what my clothes looked like.
But the world may be a better place because
I was important in the life of a child.

Children Learn What They Live

If a child lives with criticism
They learn to condemn.

If a child lives with hostility
They learn to fight.

If a child lives with ridicule
They learn to be shy.

If a child lives with shame
They learn to feel guilty.

If a child lives with tolerance
They learn to be patient.

If a child lives with encouragement
They learn confidence.

If a child lives with praise
They learn to appreciate.

If a child lives with fairness
They learn justice.

If a child lives with security
They learn to have faith.

If a child lives with approval
They learn to like themself.

If a child lives with acceptance and
friendship
They learn to have loving
relationships in the world.

Anonymous

**Compliments of
Who's Schooling Who?
www.wisw.net
info@wisw.net**

✂ Cut Here and Paste on Cardboard

Children Learn What They Live

If a child lives with criticism
They learn to condemn.

If a child lives with hostility
They learn to fight.

If a child lives with ridicule
They learn to be shy.

If a child lives with shame
They learn to feel guilty.

If a child lives with tolerance
They learn to be patient.

If a child lives with encouragement
They learn confidence.

If a child lives with praise
They learn to appreciate.

If a child lives with fairness
They learn justice.

If a child lives with security
They learn to have faith.

If a child lives with approval
They learn to like themself.

If a child lives with acceptance and
friendship
They learn to have loving
relationships in the world.

Anonymous

**Compliments of
Who's Schooling Who?
www.wisw.net
info@wisw.net**

Keep One and Share One with a Friend